Between a

CHURCH

and a

HARD PLACE

AVERY

a member of Penguin Group (USA) Inc.

New York

Between a

CHURCH

and a

HARD PLACE

One Faith-Free Dad's

Struggle to Understand

What It Means

to Be Religious

(or Not)

ANDREW PARK

Published by the Penguin Group
Penguin Group (USA) Inc., 375 Hudson Street,
New York, New York 10014, USA • Penguin Group (Canada),
90 Eglinton Avenue East, Suite 700, Toronto, Ontario M4P 2Y3, Canada
(a division of Pearson Penguin Canada Inc.) • Penguin Books Ltd, 80 Strand, London
WC2R 0RL, England • Penguin Ireland, 25 St Stephen's Green, Dublin 2, Ireland
(a division of Penguin Books Ltd) • Penguin Group (Australia), 250 Camberwell
Road, Camberwell, Victoria 3124, Australia (a division of Pearson Australia
Group Pty Ltd) • Penguin Books India Pvt Ltd, 11 Community Centre,
Panchsheel Park, New Delhi–110 017, India • Penguin Group (NZ),
67 Apollo Drive, Rosedale, North Shore 0632, New Zealand
(a division of Pearson New Zealand Ltd) Penguin Books
(South Africa) (Pty) Ltd, 24 Sturdee Avenue, Rosebank,
Johannesburg 2196, South Africa

Penguin Books Ltd, Registered Offices: 80 Strand, London WC2R 0RL, England

First trade paperback edition 2011
Copyright © 2010 by Andrew Park

Most Avery books are available at special quantity discounts for bulk purchase for sales pro-
motions, premiums, fund-raising, and educational needs. Special books or book excerpts also
can be created to fit specific needs. For details, write Penguin Group (USA) Inc. Special
Markets, 375 Hudson Street, New York, NY 10014.

The Library of Congress has catalogued the hardcover edition as follows:

Park, Andrew.
Between a church and a hard place: one faith-free dad's struggle to understand what it
means to be religious (or not) / Andrew Park.
p.   cm.
ISBN 978-1-58333-371-6
1. Families—Religious life.   2. Fathers—Religious life.   I. Title.
BL625.6.P37   2010   2009047664
204'.41—dc22
[B]

ISBN 978-1-58333-417-1 (paperback edition)

Printed in the United States of America
1   3   5   7   9   10   8   6   4   2

Book design by Susan Walsh

While the author has made every effort to provide accurate telephone numbers and Internet
addresses at the time of publication, neither the publisher nor the author assumes any
responsibility for errors, or for changes that occur after publication. Further, the publisher does
not have any control over and does not assume any responsibility for author or third-party
websites or their content.

---

*Penguin is committed to publishing works of quality and integrity.
In that spirit, we are proud to offer this book to our readers;
however, the story, the experiences, and the words
are the author's alone.*

In memory of my parents

CONTENTS

Wouldn't it be weird if you died, and you woke up, and you were in heaven, just like they always told you? And everybody had wings on, and the pearly gates? Wouldn't you feel *stupid*?

—STEVE MARTIN

[*one*]

CHAPEL CHAT

My son was three years old the first time I heard him say "God."

He didn't get it from me.

Cristina and I had recently enrolled him in preschool at a Methodist church a short drive from our house. We'd had him in a program three mornings a week at another church near our house, also Methodist—*Welcome to the Bible Belt!*—until the day I arrived early for pickup and found him on one of the playground benches, curled up as if back in the womb and unable to explain what had caused this despair. The incident, the last in a long string of red flags since a new teacher had arrived that fall, had provided our first experience with the brand of parental guilt that keeps you awake at night, wondering how you turned out to be such an awful person that you would consider outsourcing the rearing of your child for even one second. For a couple of months after that, we kept him home. Eventually, though, we'd had to acknowledge that the boy had taken well to the stimulation and structure preschool offered, and now that we had another child, his mother needed a break from full-time parenting. This new batch of Methodists seemed like good people who would care for him properly. But there was one hitch: Once a week the kids were lined up and led from their classrooms to the sanctuary for a short religious lesson the preschool called "Chapel Chat."

Now, my wife and I had for the most part avoided chapels since becoming adults. And the last thing we wanted to do was chat in one. We didn't belong to any church, and our feelings about organized religion, like our feelings about organized labor and organized crime, were, at best, ambivalent. We found all three were best experienced only as part of Hollywood movies. But that left us in a pickle: So that we could care for my elderly father and be near old friends, we had recently moved back to the midsized North Carolina city in which I had grown up, a place where nine out of ten preschools were run by churches. When touring these facilities, our first question for the directors was always whether they subjected the children to any of that, you know, Jesus stuff, and to our surprise, not that many did. I suppose it made sense in a competitive market to stay as secular as possible. But it was midway through the academic year and most of the good programs (and by "good," I mean ones where you didn't feel the need to make unannounced visits to make sure your son wasn't being left to wallow in a puddle of his own misery while the other children were playing on the monkey bars) were already full. Knowing we were lucky to find an opening at this one, we decided to take our chances.

To our relief, our son adapted well to his new environment, and, for the most part, it wasn't much different from the old one. At this program, instead of having to come inside to pick up our children, we parents lined up in our station wagons and minivans and one by one the kids came running out to greet us. The new routine seemed to make our son feel a bit more grown-up, and as he warmed to his new teachers, we began to feel like we had atoned for the earlier debacle. That is, until that day, when we were reminded of the fragility of parental success, not to mention how uneasy the topic of religion made us both.

We were sitting on the ell-shaped couch in our den, passing the time in one of the amazing yet quickly forgotten ways that you do when your free hours are given over to bringing up small children, when His name came out of his mouth. Our reaction was approximately the same as if the word had been "antediluvian" or "nanotechnology." Like most parents, we greeted every new addition to his vocabulary with a glee that would make innocent bystanders gag. But this one came out of nowhere, and I had no idea how to react. I wanted to grab it out of the air and gently shove it back into his mouth for a few more years. The context in which he said it was never clear. It just kind of spilled out, but neither of us had any doubt it was Yahweh's nickname that had breached his perfect lips. I said nothing, my wide eyes fully expressing my internal alarm. Cristina remained calm, the way you would if a kid was test-driving a bad word picked up at school and you were afraid an overly animated reaction might encourage him to add it to his everyday conversation.

—Do you know who God is? she asked him gently.

—Yes. God makes us.

His matter-of-fact response indicated that the answer was so obvious as to be a priori. Cristina glanced at me but decided to ignore the panic now erupting visibly all over my face. She turned back to him and tried probing a bit deeper.

—How does God make us?

Again, he knew the answer, and he delivered it with the confidence that comes with knowing something is the undisputed truth.

—He screws on our heads and pops in our eyeballs.

Upon hearing this, my worry subsided a bit. Whatever he had picked up at preschool was too absurd to be of any harm. In the days to come, I delighted in passing on this adorable little anecdote to friends and relatives.

But before long, from his crude initial hypothesis, my

son began to formulate what is referred to in religious literature as a "Christian worldview." His mind was made up about the existence of God. And how. But the details still tripped him up. For instance, he wondered why there was a "big X" on the top of churches we passed while driving in the car.

Cristina and I tried to respond by balancing our own lack of traditional belief with a sincere appreciation for his curiosity. Independently, we each decided that all discourse about matters of faith should be prefaced by the phrase "Well, some people believe . . ." This seemed like a sensible disclaimer that would help him understand that absolute truth is an elusive thing in the world into which he had been born. But we both knew full well we were just trying to buy some time until we had something more definitive to tell him or at least thought him mature enough to accept our squishiness. We knew that he didn't care about "some people." He wanted to know what we, his parents, believed, what to us was true, what to us was real. But we couldn't tell him. We were as reluctant to say something that would stifle his thought as we were to let him believe everything that the Methodists told him. For a while, as a compromise, we tried substituting "Mother Nature" for God. This, too, struck us as quite sensible: We both loved nature, wanted our children to appreciate and respect it, too, and liked the idea of a little pro-woman affirmative action in the supernatural realm. But ultimately she proved no better than the Man Upstairs. She was a poor proxy, only prompting more questions we couldn't seem to answer. In actuality, they were the same questions, just with a different omniscient, omnipresent deity making mysterious decisions, like letting a good person do a bad thing or a flower die or one animal savage another for food. We were usually successful in directing the conversation elsewhere, but that tactic only lulled us into thinking we were addressing the issue when we weren't, making his inevitable inquiries just as startling the next time they came round. If we couldn't answer even a simple question, someone else certainly would. At this rate, he'd be born-again before he got to kindergarten.

One evening after bedtime, I heard soft chatter coming from the room he shared with our daughter, who was one at the time. I continued down the hall, stopping short of the door until I could hear what was being said. The boy, lying awake in his miniature bed, was trying to share some explosive new information with his sister, but she was already asleep in her crib on the opposite side of the room.

—Hey, did you know that God made us?

He paused, but there was no answer.

—And when we die, we go back to Him?

His voice rose expectantly at the end of his question in

anticipation of an awestruck response, but once again, none came.

—Isn't that so cool?

I lingered by the door a moment, expecting a return of the panic that had visited me on the couch. But it never showed. In its place, a different feeling arose, something vaguely happy, maybe even hopeful. For a moment, I felt his wonder at the idea of a benevolent creator just waiting to welcome us back into His loving, secure embrace. I understood his comfort at the notion of a grand plan for our existence. When you put it that way, it *is* so cool. I've just never believed it.

] [

I am not an atheist. Correction: I've never thought I was an atheist. To me, atheism is so final, and unnecessarily so, like walking out on *The Empire Strikes Back* before Darth Vader has dropped the "I'm your father" bomb on Luke. No, I've always been one to stay until the credits roll, withhold judgment until all the facts are in, keep all my options open. I saw no reason not to hedge my metaphysical bets, too. The trouble is, as labels go, the alternatives aren't much better. *Agnostic? Irreligious? Unbeliever?* Um, no. These are not ear-pleasing names. In fact, they're borderline profane. They drip with a negativity that implies I'm a nonperson lacking in something fundamental to human nature. *Heretic? Apostate? Infidel?* Ouch. Okay, maybe those first three aren't so bad. Thank God I didn't live during the Middle Ages. What else you got? *Freethinker?* Too smug. *Bright?* Too silly. And too smug. *Secular humanist?* They still have those? *None of the above?* Now we're getting somewhere.

For as long as I can remember, I've thought of faith as something other people had. Simple as that. It's difficult to describe what it's like not putting my trust in religion, not thinking that the divine is real and worthy of my mind's attention, much less its devotion or worship. It's not that I necessarily disbelieve such things. It's just that the space that in some people contains belief and in others disbelief has in me always been somewhat barren, filled only with fleeting, tentative guesses that blow through like discarded candy wrappers—a vacant lot between everyone else's seeming towers of certainty: Who would want to hang out there for long? Better to avoid it. Which is what I've always done.

But a funny thing happened on the way to becoming a thirtysomething father of two: I started to question whether I had really thought this position all the way through. At least for the time being, Cristina and I were responsible for all aspects of our children's lives, including their spiritual guidance. For better or worse—and trust me when I tell you that most people have an opinion as to which it is—we had opted them out of religion, organized or otherwise. If "unbelief is as much of a choice as belief is," as the theologian Frederick Buechner has argued, then by doing absolutely nothing, we had made up our little family's mind already. Was I in danger of failing my children, of neglecting to prepare them for life in every way that I could, of sucking at being a dad? There seemed to be certain perks to faith that don't come packaged so neatly in any other form: community, identity, fellowship, introspection, ethics. I had missed out on that package. Was it fair to deprive my kids of them, too? Sure, this might win me friends among those who liken instilling religious faith in your progeny to abusing them. But one day over coffee in her kitchen, my aunt Susie, a proud and devoted Episcopalian for more than fifty years, warned me of the opposite. To fail to take children to church was to deny them comfort, security, and self-worth. People who grow up without religion lack self-esteem, she said.

Trouble was, I wasn't really the right person to prepare them in this particular regard. Penmanship I can do. Early REM I've got covered. Free throws are no problem. Religion? Not my strong suit. Still, I found myself wondering why exactly I was maintaining this "Don't ask, don't tell" policy on matters of faith, like they were radioactive and my children should never be exposed to them. Had I grown up in a different family, a more pious family, the silent treatment I was giving to religion might constitute a principled stand that proved I was my own man, unyoked from heredity or tradition. Instead, I worried that my faith-free existence, because I had never really questioned it, was somehow *less* principled, less defensible. I found myself looking at my churchgoing neighbors with envy, as if the simple act of getting everyone dressed up and in the SUV in time for eleven-o'clock services once a week was proof that they had it all figured out in the parenting department. I felt jealous of people who could say "I'll keep you in my prayers" or "God bless you" or "Godspeed" without irony. I wanted to curse my intellectualizing, my skepticism, my lack of any mystical feelings. I fretted that I was ultimately consigning my two young children to the same confusion as their poor pitiful father, and for no reason other than I hadn't gotten around to overcoming this squeamishness about spirituality and doing something about it. I could just imagine the look on their faces when the End Times come. Armageddon is nigh, just like the Left Behind novels said, and all the righteous kids are on the express ride to heaven to get their holy lovin' Rapture on. Their faces full of hope, my children turn to me and ask if they can go, too, but I'm too preoccupied with rummaging through the kitchen drawers for a flashlight that works to answer. "Sorry, kids," I'll tell them later, as our apocalyptic future begins to come into focus. "Daddy's been busy."

] [

I've been to church. Plenty of times. My kids have been, too. One of them has even been blessed by a man of the cloth. But in the last fifteen years, my visits to houses of worship have been mostly for weddings or funerals or Christmas Eve services, when all my favorite songs get played. On the Friday after 9/11, I went, like most of America, ducking into a downtown chapel with Cristina and a coworker, but that was as far as it went. Yet I have no problem with church. Belief was what confounded me. Naturally, I blame my parents. Belief, fate-changing, earth-quaking, mind-altering belief, could have been my birthright. My great-grandfather, the closest thing to a patriarch my family had, devoted his life to his faith, helping establish the fastest-growing denomination in the fastest-growing religious faith in the world—Pentecostalism. Near the end of his life, he met Oral Roberts, who was then a barnstorming young faith healer and not yet the world-famous televangelist I remember from the mid-1980s asking his followers for $8 million to prevent God from "calling him home." Hoping he might cure his failing kidneys, my great-grandfather asked Roberts to lay hands on him, but the preacher refused. "Mr. Culbreth," he said. "I am not worthy."

] [

That story would be repeated often in my family, until, like most of my great-grandfather's accomplishments, it was imprinted in our lore. His faith, however, didn't turn out to be indelible. By the time I came along, it was no longer in the family, like the heirloom lamp that is lost in a move or mistakenly put out for a garage sale. In April 1966, three months before my parents married in the living room of my uncle and aunt's house in Raleigh and then headed west for graduate school, the cover of *Time* asked in ominous red-on-black type, "Is God Dead?" It would sure seem that way to me. My parents were intellectual, cultured, politically liberal. Religion didn't have much relevance for them. It had lost whatever truth and meaning it once had. When I was born, instead of Protestant or Catholic or Jew, they checked "No, thanks" and went about raising my brother and me, deities not included. My parents never told me if they believed in God or if I should.

They didn't send me to Sunday school or read to me from the Bible. At holiday dinners, my father might say a blessing before we dug in, but that was the extent of it. We seemed to have little need to talk about religion, at least not in any serious way. And then one day, my brother declared himself an Evangelical Christian, and it became almost the only thing we could talk about, the eight-hundred-pound messiah in the corner we feared would tear our family apart. There's an old adage about the fleeting nature of family wealth: "Rags to riches to rags in three generations." In four, we had made it from Holy Roller to Heathen and back to Holy Roller. May the circle be unbroken.

] [

There are two topics that couples are advised to discuss in depth before getting married: money and religion. Cristina and I ignored this advice. At the time of our wedding eleven years ago, our financial situation was far too scary to discuss: We owed $20,000 on our credit cards, more than twice that in student loans taken out to attend journalism school, and, as was mentioned repeatedly at our wedding, including during the minister's homily, I had no job. (In my defense, I had gallantly followed my betrothed to Texas so she could stay near her family, but this didn't seem to matter to anyone old enough to matter.) Cristina shared my deficit in the faith department, too. Shortly before the big day, it was suggested we take a quiz that would measure our compatibility on a range of issues that often cause problems for newlyweds. Asked about the role that faith would play in our life together, we both gave the same response—"uncertain." *Total compatibility!* As for the actual ceremony, which took place on the grounds of a lovely Austin art museum, we were characteristically laissez-faire. A person of the cloth to officiate seemed inescapable, so we chose a liberal Methodist pastor whom Cristina had interviewed for an article in the local alt-weekly. We didn't write our own vows, but we did balance the customary reading from 1 Corinthians 13 with "The Master Speed" and an Apache love poem. The rest we left up to her. Just don't make it too *Jesus-y*, we pleaded.

Cristina's family is Catholic. Well, it *was* Catholic. She and her four siblings grew up in the Church, but today they range in belief from her atheist younger sister to an older brother who is, like mine, born-again. Her mother, who grew up in Madrid in the days of Franco, is the only one in the family who still claims fealty to the Vatican (as does an uncle back in Spain who occasionally expresses long-distance concern for the fate of our immortal souls). But Cristina was baptized, and when she turned seven, she wore a special white dress for her First Communion. She

went to parochial schools and to mass
on the weekend, too. Her memories o
different from mine, are by and large f
met, she could still marvel at how the
didn't spend much time reading the B

Jesus the way Protestants did. But if being a part of the
Church had given her world structure and social outlets
when she was a child, it did little more for her when she
became an adult. The older she got, the more her bemuse-
ment at what she saw as its quirks—"They did away with
limbo? Really?"—turned into irritation with its orthodoxies,
irritation that began to eat away at her commitment. On
birth control, homosexuality, the role of women, the Church
was wrong, in her opinion. The horrifying revelation that
the monsignor of her school had molested friends of hers
would have been the last straw, but by then she had tried
and failed to make peace with her former faith. She had
even gone to mass at several different churches when she
was pregnant with our daughter, our son in tow, hoping to
regain some of her former devotion, but each time it was
no use: The priest attempted too many sports analogies, or
the architecture was too modern, or some snotty woman
wouldn't make room for her in the pew. At the baptism of
a Catholic friend's child, she was stunned hearing the dark
questions posed during the ceremony:

    —Do you reject Satan?

And all his works?

—Do you reject sin, so as to live in the freedom of God's children?

—Do you reject the glamour of evil and refuse to be mastered by sin?

—Do you reject Satan, father of sin and prince of darkness?

Catholic baptisms are occasions for the entire congregation to renew its vows to the Church, which is why they are often held during mass. But upon hearing those questions, Cristina knew she couldn't do that. My wife is no Satanist, but she could not say the words honestly, nor could she agree to commit her own children to the faith. Her days as a Catholic were over.

] [

After my brother's conversion, my parents and I joined a church, as much as a safe haven as anything else. But even though I came to love the community there, I was by then in late adolescence and largely immune to the theology. Witnessing the change in my only sibling and my parents' unhappy reaction had made me wary of spiritual transformation. It still does. In truth, all of the questions that force us to consider how we got here and why and what will happen when we die have always made me uncomfortable. They're scary. They have no answer. To me, it has always been less frightening to believe that our place in the universe is the result of a certain amount of randomness. This belief in nothing, this attachment to no faith or creed, has served me well, thank you very much. I'm a good person. I've got a moral compass. The golden rule, it seems to me, covers most of it. I'm kind to strangers and old ladies and puppies. I've tried to be charitable and forgiving and humble and loving in my lifetime, and my most prominent failures to do so still eat at me to this day. Impure thoughts? Yes, I've had a few. Lust in my heart? At times. Taken the Lord's name in vain? I long ago adopted my mother's habit of exclaiming "Gawd almighty" anytime I felt even mild disgust. It's funny. But from where I stand, these represent little more than misdemeanors in the cosmic scheme of things. I know I'm an unlikely candidate for conversion. I'm a Democrat. I subscribe to *The New York Times*. I listen to public radio. In my Volvo. Often while drinking a latte. And if that weren't enough, I'm a member of a profession that prizes skepticism above all else. Recently, when I pitched a New York magazine editor on an article I hoped to write about the scientific roots of religion, he warned me that it would be a tough sell since all of the top people on the masthead were atheists. Another query, this one about one church's sophisticated market research, was turned down by an editor weary of the prominent role faith had assumed in America under President Bush and the Religious Right. He wrote in an e-mail:

—Andrew, this is a good pitch, but I feel like I've lived that for the past eight years.

Deep down, I, too, have a bias against religion. I suppose it's inescapable. There's a file in my mind so thick with immoral, idiotic, and hypocritical acts undertaken in its name that the case should have long since been closed. The times in which I've lived have been one long Culture War, and my side was chosen for me before I was born, like a Red Diaper baby born a half-century ago.

But faith, perhaps precisely because it is alien, still holds an allure for me. Maybe it's the times in which we're living, when the world's survival seems to turn on competing interpretations of a few ancient texts. Seems like I should have an opinion myself. But more than that, there is a curiosity in me about the community religion germinates, an aspiration for the commitment it demands, a clichéd desire for something different for my children from what I had. And like most Americans, I am not far removed from people for whom faith was an intense, life-directing force. I have memory—both brain and blood—of men and women thrusting violently to the extremes of the spiritual spectrum. Some repudiating the faith of their fathers as too liberal and permissive, others rejecting it as too rigid and archaic. Some accepting the unseen without question and then suddenly turning their back on it, others doing the opposite. Some feeling nothing for God and then being brought suddenly to their knees, others being cursed with travails that undermine long-held trust, still others being faced with mortality and desperately wanting there to be more.

This is not a story about struggling with God; it's about struggling with whether to struggle with God. It's about the pros and cons of taking a leap of faith at a frighteningly uncertain time in the perilous occupation of modern dad. It's about trying to open my mind to religion without corrupting my sacred secular principles, about reconciling the belief and disbelief I have seen, about coming to grips with the conflicting views of Christianity running through both my nature and my nurture. At some point after hearing my son utter one simple word, I resolved to take the most serious issue humans face a bit more seriously. I decided I needed to go to extremes. I got to know today's Evangelical celebrity preachers. I read parts of the Bible and back issues of *Christianity Today*. I even flipped through the colorful and informative brochures left by the Jehovah's Witnesses. My goal was simply to level the playing field a bit so that I might stake out some defensible middle ground for me and my family. Middle ground isn't exactly a popular place these days. The overreaching of the Religious Right is well known, so much so that it seems recently to have backfired. But there was an unctuousness about atheists these days, too, these know-it-alls with their flying spaghetti monsters and de-baptism ceremonies, shooting Jesus fish by the barrelful. I got the joke, but it had gotten old quick. I wanted to believe there was another option out there.

] [

Not long after we moved back to Charlotte, I met up with Chris, an old college friend who had grown up there, too. Chris and I shared many of the same interests—music, politics, travel—but his traditional Catholic upbringing had always divided us. His father had attended mass every day for the last forty years. Once, on a long, dark drive home for Thanksgiving in his silver hatchback, he had defended his family's faith as having, if nothing else, "an answer to the most important question in the world." It was a powerful argument for which I, tellingly, had no rebuttal. I wasn't even sure what question he was talking about. Still, I never thought of Chris as particularly religious: He did not, as far as I know, regularly attend church, wasn't involved in religious groups on campus, and certainly didn't refrain from typical college activities of which the pope was known to disapprove. But in the intervening fifteen years, he had come to rely on his faith as a constant, no matter where his itinerant existence took him. He was dating a fellow Catholic whom he would later marry, and organized religion was becoming increasingly prominent in his life, or at least so it would seem by the question he popped after we had sat down to eat.

—So, what are you doing faith-wise?

Faith-wise? This was a variant on a question I had heard frequently since starting a family and moving to a new place:

—Have you picked a church yet?

Or:

—Have you found a pastor you like?

Or, occasionally:

—How are you planning to raise the children?

—*To keep questions like that to themselves.*

But Chris had asked the question out of genuine interest, and I felt obliged to answer it honestly. He knew my family's history and that I had long struggled with questions of faith. He didn't know that they had reared their head again with the arrival of children. I divulged to him my growing concern that I had no answer for my kids and that they would soon be at the age at which they would want and need one. He told me directly that I needed to have an answer for myself first, that it was part of my personal evolution that I had to undertake, whether or not it yielded something I could pass along to my children. I agreed, though I was more skeptical of my chances of resolving that in the time I had before the questions began.

—Let me ask you this. Where is your mother right now?

I paused before answering. What exactly did he mean? The moment when he warmly pulled me out of the receiving line after her memorial service to give me a bear hug flashed in my mind. In a cold March drizzle following her last stand against breast cancer, we had sprinkled small handfuls of her ashes in a flower bed underneath the church's columbarium. The rest remained in a cross-emblazoned pewter urn hidden away somewhere in my house while it awaited some cathartic treatment that never came. For the first few years after her death, I communed with her memory as I lay awake in bed at night, but I was under no illusion that this little ventriloquist act had served any purpose other than to soothe my grief at her loss, and it really hadn't occurred to me that she might have taken up residence anywhere other than in my subconscious. It took me long enough to deal with the fact that she was gone. When people reassure me that she's in heaven, joined now by my father, I have to laugh, since I don't imagine either of them believed such a place existed, and at this point, I don't believe it, either. Not really seeing how the question was relevant to what I was doing faith-wise, I turned the conversation in a different direction.

When we finished our beers, Chris and I tripped out of the bar, joking about how our college friends would laugh if they knew he was now doling out spiritual guidance. Then, as we parted ways, he startled me once again.

—I think the reason this is on your mind is that God is speaking to you. He's trying to tell you something.

I stood there for a few seconds, unsure how to respond.

Oh, boy, I thought. *This is more serious than I ever imagined.*

[*two*]

THE TWELFTH
MOST POPULOUS NATION
ON EARTH

I'm sitting at my desk in the spare bedroom that serves as my home office, tapping the button on the keyboard with the little gray picture of a loudspeaker.

—*Pipe down,* I tell the emo soundtrack playing in my headphones. *Must have near silence.*

One more tap until the lyrics are too faint to notice.

—*Now, think back, Andrew. God must have been there somewhere.*

Plumbing my childhood memories for belief in a higher power isn't exactly easy. For some reason, the first thing that comes to mind is the day I learned the truth about Santa Claus. I don't recall how the subject came up, only that as soon as it did, I was swept out the front door with my mother, my brother yelling delightedly from the stoop that now might be a good time to explain to me the birds and the bees, too. The harried reaction indicated that my parents believed they had some time before they'd have to have this discussion with me, but parents can never predict when they'll be put in such spots. We climbed into the red VW microbus, and as soon as we had gotten out of our cul-de-sac, she laid it on me. I must have been surprised, but I don't recall being too upset. I guess I knew my parents would keep the presents coming. I changed the topic to the birds and the bees and got a quick explanation that babies don't actually come from storks, another fact of life that, while surprising, I supposed I could live with. Was God mentioned in this short lesson? No. In my family, a supreme being guiding the reproductive process was no more part of reality than a red-suited fat man from the North Pole.

Anything else?

We had a Children's Bible with a marbled brown cover and cheesy drawings that my mother's mother had given us. And my grandparents in Scotland had sent my brother and me tiny baby-blue leatherette New Testaments that I thought looked very grown-up. But neither one ever came off the shelf.

—*Surely that can't be it.*

My favorite movie was *Oh, God!* I loved John Denver. And that George Burns? A scream.

—*Try again.*

Okay, when I was six or seven and started having trouble falling asleep at night, my mother sat on the edge of the bed and had me repeat after her: "Now I lay me down to sleep, I pray the Lord my soul to keep, and if I die before I wake, I pray the Lord my soul to take."

—*That's odd. Wasn't she an atheist?*

Well, obviously not. But keep in mind, she was just trying to help me get to sleep. I don't think she had religious reasons for suggesting I pray, if that's possible. For a time, I would say these lines as I lay awake, and it quelled whatever nighttime anxieties I was having. But doing so didn't make me much of a believer in a higher power. Even at that age, I questioned whether anyone was really listening.

I had a natural curiosity about church. Around the same time, my grandfather died, and I pleaded with my mother to let me attend the memorial service. I barely knew the man, an old cuss who had left my grandmother when he retired and moved to the beach so he could go fishing every day. But somehow I had a mental picture of where last respects would be paid to him—the high-ceilinged sanctuary, the impossibly long aisle, the soaring altar—and I wanted to see it in person. At that age, the only house of worship I had been inside was the local Unitarian church, an angular brown brick place tucked in thick woods. If asked about my family's religious affiliation, I would sometimes claim it as our spiritual home, but that was putting it generously. I had attended preschool there alongside other children from progressive families (it was the first preschool in the city to integrate), but we went to church there only a few times. I learned recently that my mother had found Unitarians just as smug as more conservative churchgoers. For her, even a religion with an amorphous and flexible spirituality and deemphasis of God was a faith too far.

Still, I never felt we were much different from other families. I certainly never knew we were living outside the mainstream of America. My parents hadn't been hippies or radicals or sexual revolutionaries. They didn't smoke pot or go to key parties. My father had emigrated from Scotland, made second lieutenant in the U.S. Air Force, lived in Germany for a time, and been married once before, to the daughter of a Congregationalist preacher (they didn't go to church, either). My mother had worked for several years as an editor for the National Education Association in Washington, stood five feet eleven, and had a sharp wit that belied a delicate frame. My parents met at a cocktail party, the host of which neither of them knew. They had my brother in 1967 and me in 1970, just as my father was finishing his coursework for a Ph.D. in German. He wouldn't complete his dissertation, a treatise on the Marxist playwright Ernst Toller, for several more years, but when I was a year and a half old, he took a job as an assistant professor at a new campus of the public university system back in my mother's home state of North Carolina. After finishing her master's in English literature, she joined him on the faculty as a part-time lecturer, teaching freshman English and composition.

Charlotte in the early 1970s was a hotbed of faith. It was known as "a city of churches," and indeed there seemed to be one on every corner. Billy Graham had been born there and was a frequent presence, and not long after we arrived, Jim and Tammy Faye Bakker showed up to launch their nationally syndicated TV show. But like many fast-growing New South cities, Charlotte was also large and modern enough to accommodate the unchurched. We moved into a modest two-bedroom contemporary in a neighborhood where many of my father's university colleagues also lived. Their children were my earliest playmates, and most of us went to a public school that was experimenting with "open education," which meant that we learned at our own pace, called our teachers by their first names, and were encouraged to explore our creativity. These schools, which happened to be racially diverse, satisfied my parents' strong interests in education and equality, a combination that my brother mused recently might have been the crux of the spirituality in which we were raised. Yet almost by definition, kids at these schools—like the children of academic types—weren't as likely to be taken to church. There were exceptions, but even in those families, religion didn't seem to have a prominent place in the daily lives of the parents or the kids. They weren't religious, they were relig-*ish*.

The rest of us were with our parents in spiritual exile. Our moms and dads were lapsed Catholics, disillusioned Protestants, secularized Jews. My parents rarely talked about the religion in their pasts. I knew simply that they had both been brought up in faiths—my mother in the mainstream Protestantism of the South, my father in the Church of Scotland—but left them behind when they reached adulthood. To me, this seemed like the natural order of things for a couple of well-educated, well-traveled, worldly people who came of age at a time of immense social change, and my sense was always that their rejection of religion was thoroughgoing and final. As for us kids, we were too busy with the typical kid stuff to care. I took piano lessons, played T-ball and basketball, and tended my collection of Matchbox cars. I was, like my brother, tall and gawky and teased for being little more than skin and bones, a good student but not quite the young intellectual he was. Starting about fifth grade, self-conscious and eager to fit in with the most popular kids, I began mimicking their preppy fashions. My mother reminded me that we couldn't really afford Izod shirts on the salary of a state employee, but I wasn't deterred, making do with what was on the sale racks at the L & S Prep Shop. It wasn't until later that I began to think that fitting in required going to church, too.

] [

Ask someone who is not religious about religion in America
and you'll likely hear that we have witnessed a veritable
devotion explosion during the last generation. In every
other Western industrialized democracy, the pews have
been emptying for three decades, but in the United States,
the faithful have been ascendant, enlarging their influence
in politics, business, media—indeed, in all spheres of our
society—as an Evangelical wave crested over America toward the end of the twentieth century. Today, 94 percent
of Americans believe in God or some higher power or universal spirit, according to a Gallup poll, and 42 percent
of Americans say they attend church weekly or almost
weekly. "The resurgence of religion has been one of the
most striking and dramatic phenomena of our time," the
German newsmagazine *Der Spiegel* wrote in 2007. Or, as
Sam Harris wrote in his bestselling *Letter to a Christian
Nation*: "As is well known, the beliefs of conservative
Christians now exert an extraordinary influence over our
national discourse—in our courts, in our schools, and in
every branch of government."

But the state of faith in America today is actually much
more complicated than that. That's because, at the very
same time that millions of Americans have been getting
religion, millions more have been losing it, and at an even

faster pace. And just as Harris warns that faith has become too influential in American society, critics on the other side can cite statistics to argue just the opposite. Take pollster George Barna, a Christian who has made surveys of "church attendance and avoidance" a centerpiece of his work for a quarter-century. In 2007, about one-third of people he polled hadn't been to church in the last six months save for a wedding or a funeral. *Guilty!* That meant there were some 73 million Americans with little commitment to faith, 100 million if children and teenagers were included. Barna called these numbers "staggering" in the typically sober press release announcing his findings: "To put that figure into context, if the unchurched population of the United States were a nation of its own, that group would be the twelfth most populated nation on earth."

Barna's research is well regarded by his primary audience—pastors and church officials—and he is in constant demand as a speaker. But I was a bit unnerved by the depth of his knowledge about my people. When I reached him by phone on an early spring morning at his office in Southern California, I asked him why so much of his work has focused on people who avoid religion. It's just savvy market research, he told me. That's why "unchurched," a label that few of us to whom it applies would think to put on ourselves, is the word Barna and other Christians use. It tags us as the ones their message still needs to reach, the target for their evangelism, the growth market. To these people, the secularization of America is undeniable. Contrary to what the nonreligious might think, faith is not the driving force in society that it used to be or that it should be, Barna says, and his surveys are aimed at helping change that.

—As we look at the patterns over the last fifteen, twenty, twenty-five years, it has not gone well for Christian spirituality. Almost any group of measures you look at will suggest that.

I wasn't convinced. Look at the evidence: Evangelicals now make up a quarter of the adult population. Mega-churches are giving way to giga-churches with tens of thousands of members. Politicians fall all over themselves on the campaign trail to claim the strongest faith. During his presidency, George W. Bush, whose top advisers held weekly conference calls with Christian leaders, used his faith to justify war and said he believed the United States was in the midst of a "Great Awakening." Certainly, I was in the unchurched column. But if, as Barna claimed, there were so many others out there, why did I feel so alone?

I consulted the research collected by sociologists Barry A. Kosmin and Ariela Keysar of the Institute for the Study of Secularism in Society and Culture at Trinity College in Hartford, Connecticut. In 1990, in what was by far the largest modern study of religious affiliation in this country, Kosmin and Keysar asked more than 113,000 adults to describe their faith preference. But instead of asking them to choose from the customary list of the dominant American faiths plus catchall categories like "other" and "none of the above," they posed the open-ended question "What is your religion, if any?" Not surprisingly, they received more than one hundred different self-descriptions, from "Catholic" and "Baptist"—the two most frequent—to "Wiccan" and "Deity"—the two least. Still, the results reflected a deeply and almost uniformly religious nation: Only 8 percent claimed no religion at all. This was significantly higher than the trough of the mid-1950s yet only a few points above what surveys had found in the early 1970s. But when Kosmin and Keysar replicated their study a decade later, the number of "no religion" responses had jumped to 14 percent. Taking population increases into account, they estimated that the number of American adults who claimed no particular faith had more than doubled during the 1990s, from 14 million to nearly 30 million. In a separate question, they asked a subset to rate their general outlook as either "secular" or "religious"; an even higher proportion, 16 percent, chose the former. At the dawn of the twenty-first century, in the midst of a historic revival of Christian faith, the fastest-growing religion in America was no religion at all. "Increasingly the media ask if our data suggest the country is becoming more religious or less religious," they wrote in their 2004 book describing the results of their surveys, *Religion in a Free Market*. "In fact the answer is yes to both."

] [

The signs of this irreligious revival are everywhere: For tens of millions of Americans, weekend mornings are spent at First Church of the Snooze Bar, Chapel of the Crossword, Our Lady of the Gas-Powered Leaf Blower, or Temple NF-El. But what do we know about those outside the religious fold? Not much, despite the fact that this change has been brewing for decades. *Time's* provocative 1966 cover story wasn't about the rise of atheism as much as a new theological debate about the usefulness of traditional God concepts in modern times, but the societal changes underlying both phenomena were the same: "Secularization, science, urbanization—all have made it comparatively easy for the modern man to ask where God is, and hard for the man of faith to give a convincing answer, even to himself."

At the same time, theologians were debating the challenge of belief, social scientists were beginning to focus on the dimension of belonging. A tiny but growing number of Americans did not identify with any of the major faiths. Researchers referred to them as "Nones," because that was the answer they typically gave when asked to name their religious preference, but they weren't a large enough grouping to merit further study. In the first discussion of Nones in scholarly literature, a 1968 article in the *Journal for the Scientific Study of Religion,* University of Utah sociologist Glenn M. Vernon argued that this reductive moniker, which unfairly tagged the unaffiliated as also not religious, was partly to blame for their historic neglect and, consequently, the public's view of them was "blurred and indistinct."

The name stuck, though, and forty years later, understanding of Nones is just as muddled. We may be the fastest-growing religious classification, but as in Vernon's day, we are a "residual category," statistical detritus left behind by great waves of research on religious folks. Nones remain a catchall category, lumping together people who say there is no God and people who pray daily to one. Atheists, while growing in number and recently emboldened, still make up just 1.6 percent of the population, according to the Pew Forum on Religion and Public Life, which surveyed 35,000 American adults in 2007. Agnostics, who say it's impossible to know whether God exists, are another 2.4 percent, Pew found. Meanwhile, 70 percent of Nones believe in a supreme being or a cosmic spirit but describe their faith as "nothing in particular." Some of these people are "spiritual, but not religious," to use a phrase that has become popular to describe those interested in New Age practices and personal spirituality. But to quote Steven Waldman, most are simply "pious, but not religious," talking the talk but not walking the walk. If all of these people could agree on what they believe in, they'd have one hell of a religious movement on their hands, but that's not likely. *The Encyclopedia of Unbelief* coined an acronym, SUNINSHARFAN, to encompass all the varieties of Godlessness—Skeptic, Unbeliever, Non-believer, Irreligious, Nonreligious, Secular, Humanist, Ag-nostic, Rationalist, Freethinker, Atheist, and Naturalist or Nontranscendentalist—but as far as branding goes, I'm not sure I see it on a billboard or a bus ad. And given the lack of self-awareness of many Americans, it might not be much help. In Kosmin and Keysar's survey, one in ten families in which both parents claimed no religion also claimed they were members of a church. The Pew study found that 20 percent of self-described atheists said they believed in God, which, depending on your point of view, calls either atheists or statistics into serious question.

In the early twentieth century, the Census Bureau tal-lied Americans' religious affiliation but ended the practice in 1957 on the grounds that it violated the separation of church and state. That's left pollsters and social scientists to do it, and often they fixate on flawed measures. For in-stance, most Christians consider participation in a church to be a critical element of practicing their faith. But fewer than half of Americans consider themselves part of a particular congregation, despite their beliefs or identification with a denomination or faith, and fewer say they go to church regularly. And even those rather tepid results are controversial. In the 1990s, social scientists began to question whether "social desirability bias" caused respondents to overstate their religious activity lest they appear deviant, even in this day and age. *I mean, who hasn't fudged and said they floss every night when really it's only once every leap year?* In one study, researchers counted cars in church parking lots, estimating an average of three people per car, to get a more accurate reading of church attendance. Their finding: It was closer to one in four American adults than Gallup's two in five, and subsequent studies in which subjects were asked to keep diaries tracking their daily activities, which social scientists considered more accurate than responses to phone surveys, supported that figure. Another survey, the National Election Study, reworked its church attendance question to eliminate the potential for social desirability bias. The result: The "never" responses jumped from 12 percent to 33 percent in one year and stayed there.

Still, certain demographic traits consistently correlate with low levels of church attendance and religious identification. Ready to play "You might be a None if . . . ?" Generally, men are less religious than women. Asian-Americans are less religious than Caucasians, who are less religious than Hispanics, who are less religious than African-Americans. Single people and those living with a partner, but not divorced, are less religious than married with no children, who are less religious than married with children. Being a None doesn't make you smart, but we are more likely to have a postgraduate degree and make at least $100,000 a year. We're more likely to have emigrated from Asia, Canada, or Western Europe than from Latin America or Eastern Europe, and more likely to have moved around within the United States than to have stayed put. People on the coasts are less religious than people in the flyover states. The percentage of the population with no religion in the Pacific Northwest is so high that it has been called "the None Zone," but in Kosmin and Keysar's most recent study, taken in 2008, New England was even less religious. The states with the highest proportion of people who say that religion is an important part of their daily lives, according to Gallup Poll interviews with more than 350,000 Americans during 2008? All in the South.

Every faith has its refugees among the Nones, but former Catholics and former Jews account for much higher shares of the overall population. One theory is that cultural taboos on joining a Protestant denomination would cast them as "disloyal." Another theory is that social class plays a major role when Americans are choosing a faith, and Catholics are closer in social class to Nones than, for example, Pentecostals.

Finally, while there's no data on which professions correlate greatest with godlessness, it's a pretty sure bet that the occupation that my parents chose, teaching at the university level, would be among the highest. A recent study by the Institute for Jewish and Community Research found that 8 percent of college faculty members identified themselves as atheists, more than five times the proportion in the general public. Talk about being born under a bad sign.

] [

As I waded through all of this data, I tried to find my family. We never identified with any particular label, but we were classic Nones, defining ourselves mainly by what we were not rather than what we were. This wasn't confined to religion, either. We were not rich. We were not poor. My father was not in business, and my mother was not concerned with how much money he made. We didn't have cable. We didn't buy new cars. We didn't like football or golf and complained when either one caused *60 Minutes* to start late. Perhaps most important, we were not joiners. My mother played in a tennis league and my father was active in an association of translators of foreign lan-

guages, but other than that, we weren't members of anything: not Elks Club, not Toastmasters, not a bowling league
or a poker night or a supper club. Our focus, to para-
phrase James Dobson, was on the family. My mother took
her role as a parent especially seriously. Her children were
her purpose in life, her reason for being. She was constantly waging war against television and always kept close
watch on our teachers. She was also very concerned about
our nutrition, having read Adelle Davis's prescient books
on good eating, and did much of her shopping at the health
food store. Consequently, I wound up with carob cookies
and sesame sticks in my lunch instead of snacks that actually tasted good. While my father could be cool and reserved and reluctant to drive us too hard, she indicated
that it would be nice if at least one of us would write the
Great American Novel.

We were a loving family, but we valued humor over
most other modes of expression. While my parents would
not have approved of our mocking others' genuine faith,
we all took delight in skewering religion's excesses. My
father never failed to tell visitors from out of town that the
Bakkers' TV show, *The PTL Club,* stood for "Pass the
Loot," and groaned if someone was called a "good Christian" or a good deed was described as "the Christian thing
to do." "Christians aren't perfect, just forgiven," read the
bumper sticker my dad loved to hate. "The family that

prays together, stays together," read another. He and my mother also introduced us to Gilbert and Sullivan, *Candide,* and the nasally satirical singer from the fifties and sixties, Tom Lehrer. It was after listening to Lehrer's catchy tune "The Vatican Rag," a lampoon of the Catholic Church's attempts to make its liturgy and ritual more accessible, that I asked the meaning of the words "rosary" and "genuflect." I didn't know until much later that Catholics had wanted the song banned. "Make sure you don't play that when Murphy comes over," my dad said, referring to my mother's best friend, who had been raised Catholic, but she would have gotten the joke. Another catchy tune from Lehrer, the child of a Jewish American family, parodied the forced kindness of "National Brotherhood Week," when people were supposed to be nice to one another, despite religious and other differences; according to the song, Protestants and Catholics hated each other, Hindus hated Moslems, "and everybody hates the Jews!" I didn't know why it was funny, but it was, and I repeated it frequently. I loved it when we put the record on and stretched out in the family room together. These listening sessions were an informal part of my education. Even my young ears recognized Lehrer as a truth-teller. That he used words to highlight the absurdity of so much human behavior, including what to many people is sacred, only made him more of a hero to me. My brother and I would find the same willingness to make light of faith when we discovered the Fire-sign Theatre, Monty Python, SCTV, Woody Allen, George Carlin, and Steve Martin. It didn't matter to us that Martin turned the tables on the modern rejection of religion—"In college they told me this was all bullshit!" he imagined pleading to Saint Peter at the gates of heaven—they were our idols.

As Nones, my family and I were riding the wave of de-churching that began in the 1960s, when adherence to traditional religious teachings began to decline, social norms about regular churchgoing loosened, and external displays of piety faded. Today, the percentage of adults who report that they were raised unaffiliated with any religion is higher than the proportion raised Jewish, Episcopalian, Lutheran, Presbyterian, or Pentecostal, according to the Pew study. Considering that respondents to that survey were born no later than 1990, the beginning point for the most recent surge in the size of the nonreligious population, that figure seems likely to grow. Kosmin and Keysar predict that Nones will make up one-quarter of the American population in twenty years.

Or maybe it won't. In some countries, rising rates of secularism correlate with rates of fertility and family sizes far below those in more devout places. That would indicate that there's a demographic constraint on the future growth of the nonreligious as a percentage of the population. And while the unaffiliated category is a popular destination for those raised religious—eight in ten grew up in a faith—Pew found it had among the lowest retention rates of any grouping, with less than half of those raised without religious affiliation staying that way as adults. Just look at what happened with my brother. Indeed, of all the trends identified in studies of Nones, age is the most controversial. Generally, the young are less religious than the old. For instance, in the Pew study, the percentage of those under thirty who identified as unaffiliated was three times the proportion of those over seventy. On first blush, that would seem to be the result of a larger proportion of Americans growing up unaffiliated, like me. But it's not clear if those gaps will close as today's under-thirty set gets older and some get married and have children. In other words, researchers don't know if that's a sign of the younger generation being less religious or just being younger. "This same effect can be found in *every* national survey of church attendance ever done," preeminent sociologist Rodney Stark, director of the Baylor University Institute for Studies of Religion, wrote recently. "Young people have always been less likely to attend than are older people."

The year before we talked, Barna had retooled his research on religious participation. He wanted to account for the growing number of people he saw involved in what he called "organic faith communities," essentially any unconventional mode of religious participation, from house churches and intentional communities to workplace ministries and online worship, in addition to or in place of conventional church attendance. Barna, who wrote about changing patterns of Christian faith in his book *Revolution,* including the hunger among many younger believers for simpler, more authentic spiritual experiences than the modern church offers, has for four years led a house church consisting of him, his wife, their three adopted daughters, and three other families. To capture these people in his research, Barna replaced the churched/unchurched approach with five new categories: "Unattacheds" have not attended any kind of church in the past year, "Intermittents" have not attended in the past month, "Homebodies" have attended only a house church, "Blenders" mix alternative modes with conventional church participation, and "Conventionals" do solely the latter. What's interesting about these alternative modes of worship is that they are attracting unchurched people as well as churched, in part because there is less pressure to convert or join than in a traditional church environment, he told me. When I added up Barna's new numbers, though, the percentage of people who would fit into the old "unchurched" category hadn't really changed. But to Barna, the point is to get Christian leaders to look at people who don't practice their faith conventionally in a different light.

—I think it depends on your mind-set. Why are you engaged in ministry? If it's to bless people, if it's to help individuals to grow and mature and to find a way of connecting with God that really works in [their] life, you have to recognize that there isn't one size that fits all.

I appreciated his appeal for a humbler, more open-minded approach to the unchurched, yet I had seen plenty of ministers use his statistics to rationalize more aggressive proselytizing and ever-larger empires. I began to wonder if his research at times served the opposite of what he was advocating. Over the years, he has been accused of feeding the mentality that the main weakness of Christianity is poor marketing and that what's needed in churches is corporate-style strategic thinking and watered-down theology that will appeal to the unchurched. Some of his research—one of his studies found that divorce rates among born-again Christians were just as high as those among the general population—seems designed to produce anxiety of a kind that might lead a pastor to buy a book or attend a seminar. The first chapter of his latest book, *The Seven Faith Tribes: Who They Are, What They Believe, and Why They Matter,* is titled "America Is on the Path to Self-Destruction."

Of course, in Barna's own statistics, the unchurched share of the population hasn't changed since the mid-1990s. And yet his counterparts on the side of secularism fall prey to hyperbole just as easily. When compared with Kosmin and Keysar's findings in 2001, the Pew study showed that the growth of the unaffiliated population had slowed way down, inching up just two percentage points, to 16.1 percent, in the intervening six years. But that didn't mute the cheers from atheists, even with non-churchgoing believers far outnumbering nonbelievers in their category. The trends, they believe, are on their side. PZ Myers, an evolutionary biologist who writes a popular blog, crowed: "16.1 percent is still a minority, but keep in mind that Catholics are 24 percent of the population—we could pass them by in a few years. We're *huge* . . . and growing fast."

] [

When I was the age my children are now, my best friend was Jay, who lived up the street and around the corner. We were in preschool together and then elementary school, and both our fathers taught at the university. As young friends often do, we adopted each other's hobbies and consequently both had stamp collections. Mine filled only a couple of slim notebooks and was weighted heavily toward British and German varieties that I soaked off envelopes my dad had saved from mail received from relatives and friends. Jay had inherited a couple of phone book–sized albums filled with American stamps, but more interesting were the colorful ones bearing the acronyms SWA—for Southwest Africa—and RSA—for South Africa. Once, when he wasn't looking, I even swiped one.

That my best friend's parents started their married life in Africa was just one of many things that always intrigued me about his family. Another was that his parents had been missionaries and that his father, Ron, was a professor of religious studies. And yet they didn't go to church, either. I remembered that Ron had written a book when Jay and I were kids, and I was surprised recently to find out that it was about the challenge of teaching children about religion at a time when religion no longer seemed valid. So I e-mailed Ron and asked for a copy, and when the little green hardback arrived, I opened to the first page:

> The post-Christian age no longer dwells comfortably with the story of God. What do those of us do who are responsible for children if we neither want to introduce them to the inevitable literalism of all traditional religious education, nor take comfort in doing nothing in the area of their spiritual identity?

What indeed? With both my parents gone, I could only try to guess their reasons for raising my brother and me without religion in our lives. But Jay's parents were still alive. They had known my family as long as any of our friends. And they had thought carefully about the issues that interested me. Perhaps they could serve as a proxy to help me better understand my upbringing. So one rainy fall afternoon, I met Ron and Carol in Charlotte as they were making their semiannual trek between their cabin in Maine and their winter home in Florida.

Ron had grown up in a strict Roman Catholic family in upstate New York. In college, he converted to Protestantism but remained a remarkably devout young man, joining a confraternity associated with a monastic order and converting a closet in his house into a chapel so he and his roommate would have a special place to pray. He attended Episcopal seminary and after graduating went with his new bride, Carol, to Southwest Africa to fight the apartheid being imposed by neighboring South Africa. After a year he was ordained, serving his first Holy Communion to Herero tribespeople who had refused to be resettled to segregated townships.

But it was in Southwest Africa that Ron's religious faith began to unravel. Expecting their first child, he and Carol found themselves hesitant about baptism, and when the bishop pressured them to do it when their newborn son took ill, it only hardened their resolve to delay the rite. Two years later, back in the United States and serving as a supply priest to supplement their grad student budget, Ron felt his life-long devotion to Christianity suddenly slip out of his grasp.

—I remember very distinctly walking into the church, starting the Sunday service, and realizing, very, very dramatically in a few seconds, that these words I was saying had no meaning for me. It was gone.

Carol, who had been raised in the mainline United Church of Canada, was experiencing her own break with Christianity after becoming disillusioned with the parochialism and hypocrisy she saw in churches in Africa and back in the United States.

—I was finished with organized religion. I was just ready to say, "This is not what I want to teach my children."

But if Ron and Carol—intellectual, worldly, socially conscious—represented a new post-Christian age just as my parents had, they were in the minority when they landed in the South. They moved in to neighbors greeting them with questions about where they were planning to go to church. Even at the colleges where they taught, where there were many non-churchgoers, they sometimes felt they were on the fringe of society, and there was no one interested in discussing how to handle religion with children when you yourself weren't religious. When Carol saw other parents on the playground or at school, she avoided all talk of it. Ron, who rejected the term *atheist* because he didn't want to be defined by opposition to a worldview that was no longer relevant to him, sometimes called himself "modern," but more often than not he just kept quiet about it.

Yet as a religious studies scholar Ron couldn't exactly let it all go. He still believed that children needed guidance in how to live ethically, how to treat others and the world around them, and how to deal with death, and he recognized religion's former efficacy in these areas. He believed that to remain passive in the formation of a child's spiritual identity was an invitation to others to do it themselves. Yet he wasn't going to take his children to church just to give them a social group, which he had seen many non-churchgoing parents do, dropping the kids off for Sunday school or youth group and then heading out for coffee and the newspaper. So he began thinking about religion as one of the stories under which we live, helping us understand ourselves and our place in the world. The story of God, as he called it, was one of humanity's most powerful narratives. But he no longer believed it to be true, and he didn't believe we could live under stories that aren't true lest we develop a distorted view of fundamental human issues, yet that's exactly what most people were doing. He wanted parents to discard the story of God and replace it with tales that had less potential for harm. Hence, his book, which bore the cheeky title *Santa Claus, the Tooth Fairy, and Other Stories: A Child's Introduction to Religion.*

As parents, we allow children to live under these stories because they provide them with examples of many of the same things that the story of God does, such as love, comfort, compassion, generosity, Ron believed. But we know that kids will eventually discover that these stories aren't literally true. In fact, no child past a certain age would believe them. The same could be said of myths from ancient cultures or the story of Gilgamesh the king, whose vain search for eternal life teaches him to be content with his mortality. The story of God, by contrast, was told as the literal truth and buttressed with rituals such as bedtime prayers and grace at suppertime. Children weren't given the opportunity to discover what Ron believed was its falsity, even if they suspected it the same way they had suspected that Santa was their parents. To his dismay, the story remained intact for many of those kids well into adulthood, just as it had for him, and he often found himself in the position of having to shatter it for students. To Ron, there was no question that religion was a story that shouldn't be taken literally once a child reached a certain age, any more than the story of Santa Claus or the Tooth Fairy should. There was also no question that before long, most intelligent people would share this view and Christianity would crumble for everyone. The question was merely, what to do in the meantime?

My first reading of Ron's book, or perhaps *mis*-reading, left me hopeful. Ron seemed to feel that there was value in religion even if it wasn't true, that it could enrich the lives of young children so long as it was understood by a certain age to be merely a story. I tried to imagine my parents reading it themselves and realizing that perhaps there was still time for them to expose my brother and me to religion as a positive influence. Perhaps that was the opening that I needed to introduce Christianity to my children and let them make up their own mind. Maybe I was right to feel like I was depriving my children of something by ignoring religion, despite all of my misgivings about it. Maybe I had an ally among my parents' generation. But when I asked Ron if this was what he had been trying to say, he demurred. No, he didn't think children should be exposed to religion, even for the sake of story. He had seen the story of God do too much harm in the world. Besides, society couldn't let go of the literalist view, perhaps even less so now than when he had written his book, and liberal denominations such as Quakers and Unitarians offered nothing more than watered-down versions of the same old business. Preserving religion as mere parable was too lonely a route for most parents to take.

What, then? What had they told their children about God? What had been their response when Jay and his brother, Tim, had questions about religion? Other than a few occasions, there hadn't been any questions, and Ron and Carol spoke as if they had been quite relieved by that. Once, when he was in high school, Jay had asked a friend for a Bible as a Christmas present, but that was the extent of it as far as they knew, and they never said anything to him about it. They had told their kids the stories of Santa Claus, the Tooth Fairy, even Gilgamesh. In fact, they had an illustrated book of Bible stories when their kids were little, Carol said, though Ron quickly interjected that it had been consigned to the same fate as ours. Their "backup plan" was just to lead upstanding lives and hope their children would follow suit, what people refer to today as "modeling." And what about the other benefits of church-going? They had replaced the routine and ritual of Sunday services with their own family traditions—lighting candles and raising toasts at dinner every night, for example. They had found community during their summers in Maine and through interests such as wildlife preservation and running. And they had felt confident they could handle the rest themselves, Carol said.

—You don't just muddle through getting them clean socks. You really have to be intentional about what it is that you're doing. But I guess I didn't feel we needed the support to pass on those values through that body called the church.

Ron and Carol made a clean break with religion and never looked back. After Ron's final Sunday as a supply priest, they didn't darken the door of a church except for the occasional wedding or funeral. Never even considered it, they told me. To do so would have been hypocritical. Still, for all of Ron's interest in the religious education of his children, he had not found any replacement for the story of God. He and Carol had adopted the same live-and-let-live approach to the phenomenon of religion that seemed to be the default for irreligious liberals in the 1970s and 1980s. It was the same one that my own parents had chosen. When I asked them how would they have reacted had one of their children converted to Christianity, as my brother had, Ron said he'd have no problem as long as his son wasn't in any danger. It was natural for an adolescent to want to explore something in the culture that he hadn't been exposed to before, he said. But Carol wasn't buying that answer. Too hypothetical. She turned to him.

—How would you have felt if Tim had decided he was going to become a Catholic when he got married?

Ron allowed a momentary pause as if conceding the point and then gave me a deadpan look only an old professor could muster.

—Well, I'd make sure he had read all my stuff.

[*three*]

THIS ACT OF MIND

—Why is Jesus the only human who can come back to life?

My daughter asked this somewhat indignantly one day, as if Christ's reincarnation was not a onetime event but a super power that could be deployed at will and thus perhaps should be shared with the rest of us. I had stopped asking where my kids picked up these ideas.

—Well, sweetie, some people believe Jesus came back to life after he died, but not everyone believes that.

—Can anyone else come back to life?

—No, just Jesus.

—Well, if I were Jesus I would go to heaven and make everybody come back to life!

—Why would you do that? Why not just have everyone stay in heaven?

—Well, then, I would just make our family come back to life.

—But none of us are dead yet.

—Daaaa-ddy!

I don't know if her head was hurting from this conversation, but mine certainly was. With each successive question, we were straying farther afield from anything I knew or believed in myself. But as I think back on it, maybe there's a lesson in that for adults like me who think they need to have all the facts before any transcendence will happen. I think that's what Frederick Buechner meant when he noted, in his memoir *Now and Then*, that Jesus said that one has to become a child to enter the kingdom of heaven:

> Maybe what is good about religion is playing that the Kingdom will come, until—in the joy of your playing the hope and rhythm and comradeship and poignance and mystery of it—you start to see that the playing is itself the first-fruits of the Kingdom's coming and of God's presence within us and among us.

Reading that, I found myself wondering if it was really true. Was all that was required to believe merely a reversion to that juvenile state we all existed in before we learned too much?

] [

In the spring after my father died, I frequently found myself sitting alone on the edge of his old bed in the in-law suite we had built for him, just out of reach of stacks of boxes and piles of loose papers that threatened to swallow me whole. In 2001, he'd had a stroke that had left him unable to live alone anymore. A year later, my brother and I had sold his house and filled a large self-storage unit with books and records, foot lockers and five-drawer metal file cabinets, a slide projector, a reel-to-reel tape recorder, a curio cabinet, and countless other items boxed up and towering toward the high ceiling. The remaining hard evidence of his life—and my mother's and grandmother's, too—had been sitting in that ten-by-ten climate-controlled cell for almost six years, but now that he was gone, we could no longer justify paying the usurious monthly fee. Most of its contents went to Goodwill or the dumpster, but we had saved as many letters, photographs, and other personal mementoes as we could reasonably schlep to my house, and from time to time I would wander in and begin picking through this vast, uncatalogued archive that occupied every surface of his old bedroom like an invading army. If I spied something interesting poking out of a folder of papers, I'd attempt to dislodge it and have a look. One day, it was several pages of the crinkly onionskin my father favored for typing, long ago stapled together and now discolored like a leftover apple slice. He had entered a writing contest put on by a local literary society, and this was one of his early drafts. In blue fountain pen, he had scribbled corrections, and in pencil, a running word-count in the margin. The type was now lightly smudged. It began:

> I have never had a particular fondness for taking walks. Walking as a means of getting from one place to another I do not mind and in fact prefer in cities, where it is often faster and more comfortable than using a car. But for me the phrase "taking a walk" always evokes unpleasant memories of childhood Sundays in Scotland. Whenever the weather was reasonably bearable, we would go out after church and a heavy meal; like Sunday clothes and Sunday manners, the Sunday walk was decorous, stiff and dull. We would pass other families whose clothes and behavior we would inspect, just as they scrutinized ours. At some point in time, I swore to myself that, on achieving the age of consent, I would never again go for a walk on Sunday.

I had known since I was a child that my father had unpleasant memories of his upbringing in the Church of Scotland that had made him wary of organized religion. Reading this, I saw that the impact had been much worse than that. It had made him hate *walking*.

There are two kinds of Nones in this world: those who never went to church and those who are never going back. If I fit into the first category, my parents were squarely in the second. My mother and father were a case study worthy of Harvard Divinity School. They grew up in the same faith, Presbyterianism, and both appeared to have fled it as soon as they were out of their parents' houses. My father's childhood experience had been so harsh that well into middle age, he still saw little reason to return. My mother, by contrast, wrestled with this choice her whole life. What accounted for that difference? Was it gender? Personality? Socialization? Culture? The skepticism I felt about religion was a trait I had inherited from my parents. I needed to understand how they had come by it, too. My first clues were buried in the mess that had overtaken my in-law suite.

] [

In 1955, my mother graduated from Needham H. Broughton High School in Raleigh. That year, a Judaic studies scholar named Will Herberg published a seminal book in the study of modern faith, *Protestant-Catholic-Jew: An Essay in American Religious Sociology.* Its provocative thesis was that in the midst of a postwar boom in piety, the nation's three dominant faiths had melded into a "civil religion" that united the country. At the time, 97 percent of Americans identified themselves as Protestant, Catholic or Jew, according to a Gallup poll. Herberg believed that to be an all-time high in the nation's history, and he attributed this revival to religion's ability to serve the modern American's emotional needs: security in the face of the threat from communism; community in a society atomized by social mobility and suburbs; identity after years of assimilation. A generation before, the popularity of the freethinker movement had rendered faith passé and made celebrities out of Robert Ingersoll, the firebrand orator known as the "Great Agnostic," and Clarence Darrow, the lawyer who had defended John Scopes's right to teach evolution in a Tennessee classroom. But now, believing was back in fashion, led by the descendants of European immigrants getting in touch with their roots. "'What the son wishes to forget, the grandson wishes to remember,'" Herberg wrote, quoting a prominent psychologist.

To Herberg, religion was an indelible feature of the "American Way of Life" that had emerged so powerfully with the peace and prosperity of the 1950s, and this was the America in which my mother had come of age. Everyone went to church because it was what everyone did, and her family was no different. Her mother had fled a provincial Pentecostal upbringing and her father had little interest in churchgoing, and during the early years of their marriage, as they moved every year or so in pursuit of scarce jobs, they never joined a church. But that changed when, during World War II, they moved back to North Carolina. In October 1947, they were accepted into membership at West Raleigh Presbyterian Church, and my mother became an enthusiastic participant. She attended Sunday school and joined the youth group. At Christmas she went caroling with the pastor and his daughter. A month before her eleventh birthday, in a postcard to her mother from camp, she wrote in unruly cursive, "I pray for you every night and I surely hope God is answering them." When Billy Graham came to town a few years later, Mama was in the stands and stood up with the rest of the crowd to accept Jesus as her savior.

When I try to imagine those days in Raleigh, invariably what appears to me are scenes of joyful innocence, the cliché of American life during the 1950s. But my mother's childhood was not a particularly happy one. Her only sibling had gone off to the army when she was just seven, leaving her to shoulder the tension between their parents. She was very close with her mother, a small, quiet woman who enjoyed bridge and playing the piano, but her father was prone to verbal abuse and frequently distracted by get-rich-quick schemes. On her sixteenth birthday, he wrote a rambling, self-conscious letter on stationery in which he tried to reassure her about the purpose of life. "There is a God who is the creator of all things," he wrote. "God loves you, but you must seek him. A life of service to God and Mankind is the only way to attain lasting &

complete satisfaction and contentment." It's clear upon reading the letter that there is none of the warmth required to connect with an adolescent and assuage her worries.

When her parents moved to Michigan, where my grandfather had taken a civil service job, my mother followed, turning down a scholarship to Duke to attend a small women's college. After two years, she enrolled at the University of Michigan, where she majored in English and made a new group of friends. Together they would forgo the weekend football games to take hikes along railroad tracks, visit country cemeteries, smoke cigars, and play music, hamming it up for albums' worth of pictures. Ann Arbor was her social, intellectual, and cultural coming-out, and after a six-month tour of Europe, she took a room at the Evangeline boardinghouse in Greenwich Village, working an entry-level job in publishing during the day and warming the stools of the White Horse Tavern at night. When I asked my mother's friends from that period if they could remember her showing any interest in belief, they not surprisingly came up blank. Compared with the transformative experiences she was having, religion must have seemed of little consequence. "I don't remember your mother having any problem with religion," Brenda, one of her college roommates, wrote me, using a telling turn of phrase. My mother's best high school friend, Carolyn, with whom she remained close throughout her life, was similarly stumped:

> I can tell you I do not recall that she & I ever discussed religion, organized or otherwise. It was just not something on our radar.

And then came this:

> Of course, people compartmentalize & best friends may be unaware of certain concealments of each other, but I suspect her spiritual direction was towards appreciating and savoring the good & the beautiful of this world, loving family, home, animals, garden, human expression & creativity, particularly where she knew it best, literature.

The day that letter arrived, I wept. Carolyn had summed up my mother's character more accurately than anyone ever had. Was I surprised to learn that religion had not played a greater part in my mother's life even as a young adult? Yes, but I didn't doubt it was true.

The only thing I ever knew for sure about my mother's rejection of religion was that it was at least partly due to seeing white southern churches turn a blind eye to racial injustice in the fifties and sixties. She had left the South to go to college, and stayed away for ten years afterward, watching the civil rights movement from something of a distance. But she believed deeply in compassion and social justice. Come to think of it, that might have been why she was in exile for so long. From the first time she ordered a cup of "caw-fee" at her college dining hall, prompting a bewildered response from the Yankee behind the counter, she had to adjust to being an outsider. This relocation, coupled with her burgeoning intellect and general growing-up, must have played a role in how she saw the events engulfing the region of her upbringing, whether it was Rosa Parks's arrest for refusing to give up her seat on that Montgomery bus or Orval Faubus's defiance of integration at Central High School in Little Rock, though I can't say we ever discussed it in those terms. What I do recall her saying, though, is that white people's religious institutions had lost all credibility in her eyes by their failure to support—and for some, their resistance to—the cause of equality. At best, they weren't the bulwarks of morality they purported to be. At worst, they were complicit in crimes against humanity.

Author Reynolds Price, who grew up Methodist in North Carolina and attended the same high school as my mother (and much later was my writing professor at Duke), has described feeling a similar dismay as he came of age. In his book *Letter to a Godchild: Concerning Faith*, he writes:

Above all, for me then and truly incredible for one who was reared in the South I'd heard no syllable from any white minister who condemned, or even mentioned, American racism. (When some ministers began to show more courage a few years later, many of them discovered how quickly they could be dismissed from their segregated churches for defying the will of congregations who gave few signs of having read the gospels.)

Price also discusses the roots of his faith, and says that he suffered no loss of devotion as a result. Over the years he has written extensively about Christian spirituality and produced translations of books of the Bible. But he has never returned to church.

By the time my mother moved back to North Carolina in the early 1970s, churches there had begun to take their moral responsibility to all races seriously, and many led the charge to nurture reconciliation between whites and blacks. In Charlotte, a group of families from one of the most affluent Presbyterian churches switched their membership to a black church in a poor neighborhood, and West Raleigh Presbyterian Church reached out to African-Americans and ministered to the poor and elderly. But I suspect that, in my mother's eyes, it was too little, too late, and when confronted with opportunities to oppose unnecessary wars or support the cause of women or homosexuals, organized religion would continue to disappoint her, as it did many young Americans. The divisive issues of the 1960s eroded the moral authority of even those churches that attempted to accommodate changing mores. Some researchers argue that the relaxation of the doctrine of Catholic and mainline Protestant churches in the wake of societal change led directly to the declines in participation they suffered over the subsequent decades, since at the very same time that moderate churches were bleeding members, denominations that held steadfast to their conservatism—Southern Baptists, for example—were seeing their numbers explode. Consider the Second Vatican Council, the Holy See's attempt to modernize Catholic doctrine and liturgy, including allowing mass to be said in local languages instead of Latin and eliminating the prohibition on eating meat on Fridays. The reforms of Vatican II were cheered by many as long overdue. Yet even as they were being implemented, weekly mass attendance by American Catholics fell off a cliff, from more than 70 percent in the early sixties to 50 percent a decade later. In what had become the nation's largest faith community, that represented a decline of several million regular churchgoers. The council had decreed nothing to loosen the imperative of going to mass every weekend. But it introduced to Catholics the possibility that the Church's rules were actually not immutable, ironclad laws. Sociologist and priest Andrew M. Greeley wrote in a 2004 article in the Catholic newspaper *America*: "If it was no longer a mortal sin that would send you to hell to eat meat on Friday or drink a glass of water before receiving Communion, then were you really likely to go to hell for missing Mass on Sunday or practicing birth control to hold your marriage together?"

For my mother, and millions of other Americans, it was not the softening of doctrine that undermined the authority of religious leaders and drove them away from Sunday services. It was their failure to fight for justice and compassion the way many of their members believed Jesus would have. For all the things I didn't know, I knew that much. How long it took her to come to this decision is still unclear to me. But three decades would pass before she joined another church.

] [

As I tried to understand why some of us have no faith while so many others do, I repeatedly came across a scholarly theory known commonly as "the secularization thesis." It states that as societies become more modern they naturally become less religious. The notion has been around at least since the Enlightenment, when thinkers began to argue that the discovery of rational explanations to the mysteries of the world and the diffusion of all that knowledge would naturally lead humans to cast off their beliefs in the supernatural. Marx, Hegel, and Freud all expanded on this idea in their critiques of religion, and by the second half of the twentieth century, the coming demise of religion was simply conventional wisdom in the academic world. To most social scientists, the fact that faith was a relic of the past that modern men and women were destined to leave behind was self-evident, and disputing that would be like advocating for the horse and buggy to ride to town when there's a perfectly good Porsche sitting in the driveway.

But reality has not exactly proven the secularization thesis. While it nicely explains the contemporary loss of faith across Western Europe, there are plenty of other modern societies around the world where religion has held steady or even resurged in recent years. The rapid spread of Christianity in China, the revival of Orthodox faith in Russia after the fall of communism, the popularity of private modes of spirituality and New Age mysticism throughout the world—they all seem to fight the idea of secularization. The United States is as modern as any nation in the world, yet whether you measure by religious beliefs or affiliation, it is still remarkably religious, and more so than many less modern nations. Indeed, the persistence of widespread religiosity here has led scholars to question whether Americans are merely an exception to the secularization theory or proof that it was the wrong framework for thinking about religion and human society all along.

In the 1990s, "rational choice theory" was put forth by Baylor's Rodney Stark and others as a more plausible alternative to secularization. It casts Europe as the exception rather than the United States, arguing that the established churches that still dominate the religious landscape there have grown complacent and stale, squelching the public's interest in organized faith, whereas free-market competition among American churches produces constant innovation that taps into a natural human need for spiritual participation. Perhaps that's why we lead the world in religious switching: In Pew's study, 28 percent of those surveyed said they had traded in the faith of their childhood for another, or for none at all, during their lifetime, and when moves between Protestant sects were included, the number rose to 44 percent.

Still, not everyone is ready to let go of the secularization thesis. University of Michigan professor Ronald Inglehart and Harvard University researcher Pippa Norris argue that security, not modernity, determines how secular a society becomes. After looking at data from eighty countries, they concluded that threats to human beings' physical or economic well-being stimulate the need for religion and the existential reassurance it provides, and as those threats recede, so do religious belief and participation, but the degree of religiosity may go up or down over time, based on the conditions on the ground. What of the United States, a nation with a high degree of both security and religiosity? They attribute the difference to the relative economic insecurity that Americans experience when compared with Europeans and their generous welfare states. "The experiences of growing up in less secure societies will heighten the importance of religious values, while conversely experience of more secure conditions will lessen it," Inglehart and Norris write in their 2004 book *Sacred and Secular*.

And so the debate as to whether religion has a future in modern societies, and whether Europe or the United States is the exception, rages on. Over and over, the obituary of the secularization thesis is written, only to see the theory revived by a new round of research. Stark, writing in *What Americans Really Believe*, gripes that "somehow, American intellectuals, even those whose business it is to know about trends in American religion, just can't accept that religion isn't on its way out."

] [

The church in which my father was reared, the Church of Scotland, is actually the forebear of the church in which my mother was reared, the Presbyterian Church, the faith having crossed the Atlantic with colonists from the British Isles. Since its establishment during the Protestant Reformation, the Kirk, as it is called, distinguished itself as an austere and exacting faith, and even as late as my father's time, it offered a much harsher brand of Presbyterianism than its American offspring. Sundays were reserved for worship and nothing else; celebrating Christmas was discouraged as reminiscent of Catholic traditions, and most Scots worked on December 25 if it didn't fall on a weekend. And indeed, the only stories my father ever told about his childhood experiences with church had dark overtones. The pastors were unflinchingly strict, and their discipline put them on par with the coldest, most joyless nun or fire-and-brimstone-preaching Puritan. My father described the punishments he got for minor infractions like showing up late for Sunday school or failing to be properly attired as if they still chafed. The sole exception he ever recalled was the pastor who hadn't minded if he and his friends flew their model airplanes on Sunday, even though any kind of playing outside was a violation of the Sabbath strictures. "Let them go," he said, waving off the disapproving church scolds and giving the kids a pass.

It was a pupil of John Calvin named John Knox who helped establish the Church of Scotland, which is why Presbyterians believe that our lives on Earth are preordained and God elects only some for heaven, also known as pre-destination. That, coupled with the lousy weather—*driech* was the word my father always used to describe it—might just explain the Scots people's tendency toward fatalism. But the Kirk also championed the egalitarian ideal of education for all people, an emphasis that produced many learned figures, including one of the giants of the Enlightenment, the philosopher David Hume. Early Presbyterians "felt it incumbent upon them to see that their people were instructed; confident in the truth of their faith, they felt that every member of the Church had the right to know the foundations upon which it stood, and the Scottish people, as a whole, was better educated than most populations," according to J. D. Mackie's *A History of Scotland*.

For my father, though, church seems to have done little more than contribute to what was already a dreary childhood. Born during the Great Depression, he was an only child who wanted for warmth and attention from his father, who was the police constable in their rural village. When my father was nine, World War II began, and the frightful baying of blitz sirens became a familiar sound. Lonely at home, he overcame his innate shyness by teaching himself to dance and make other kids laugh. On Saturday nights, he'd take a girl to the country dance. On New Year's Eve, he and his friends would go from house to house, having a drink at each stop, as was customary. And on V-E night, they partied at the Albert Hall until three a.m. and missed the last bus home.

After graduating from high school, my father entered Edinburgh, the country's most prestigious university. Like my mother, he took well to the independence and stimulation that college life afforded. I have a small photograph of him standing on a sidewalk with a silly grin, a cane in one hand and a suitcase in the other, stark naked save for a trench coat that came barely to his knees. Whatever interest he had in religion took a backseat to this evident social and intellectual enjoyment. His only concern about church was whether he could fly his model airplanes on Sunday, just as it had been when he was little. Shops were closed, as were movie theaters and pubs. The public golf course was closed, too, but my father and his friends secured permission to use it and even hold contests on the Sabbath, something the soccer and cricket players couldn't do. "Things were not so constraining for aeromodelers like Bill and me," my father's friend Urlan told me. "Sunday was a flying day."

Today, the strictures are gone entirely. Sunday has become one of the biggest shopping days of the week in Scotland, and soccer matches regularly play on television. Restaurants, bars, and movie theaters are all open, as are golf courses, and the streets and sidewalks bustle and buzz all weekend long. Meanwhile, organized religion has evaporated as an influence in Scottish life. A 2002 survey estimated that the Church of Scotland was drawing just 12 percent of the population on a regular basis. That might not be the bottom, either: *The Scotsman* reported in 2008 that just one in ten Scots children from ages eleven to eighteen attended church of any kind weekly and less than one-third believed in God, and church officials were quoted as saying they were pleased that the results weren't even more dismal. "These figures show young people do have a religious sensitivity which no amount of secularization can extinguish," a spokesman for the Catholic Church said.

Just how is it that faith has plunged so far so fast in my father's native land? It remains a mystery even for those who have stuck around. I asked novelist James Robertson, whose most recent book, *The Testament of Gideon Mack*, portrays the son of a dour, authoritarian Church of Scotland minister. The protagonist jettisons his faith as an adolescent when he notices that he isn't struck down after committing sins. But he follows his father into the ministry anyway—egged on by his girlfriend, who wonders why a pastor has to believe in God in this day and age—and is eventually forced to confront his atheism and his hypocrisy. On a walk in the woods, he falls into a gorge to a certain death, only to be pulled out by the Devil, and they spend three days alone in a cave. When the conversation turns to religion in modern-day Scotland, the Reverend Mack's rescuer turns snide:

> And I like the way you deal with religion. One century you're up to your lugs in it, the next you're trading the whole apparatus for Sunday superstores. Praise the Lord and thrash the bairns. Ask and ye shall have the door shut in your face. Blessed are they that shop on the Sabbath, for they shall get the best bargains. Oh, yes, this is a very fine country.

Robertson grew up in Bridge of Allan, not far from where my father did, and thus has a deep familiarity with village life in Scotland. His parents were not particularly religious, but they had attended church regularly and sent him to a private Presbyterian school. When he was thirteen or fourteen, no longer able to square it with what he knew intellectually, he also stopped believing in God. By that time, ministers and the Kirk were both beginning to lose their influence in Scottish society, especially among young people, who were questioning the authority of all institutions. Secularization in Scotland started before that, with the psychological scars of two world wars, the rise of socialism, and the progress of science beginning to weaken the authority of organized religion early in the twentieth century, but when the 1960s arrived, the countercultural ethos emanating from America just accelerated the exodus from church. "Scottish society for three hundred, four hundred, five hundred years has had this unbelievable surfeit of hard-line religion and it's almost as if we've just shrugged it off," Robertson told me when I reached him at his home near the Scottish coast. "I suspect in our collective consciousness, there is still a feeling that actually we want to get out from under that stuff, that it actually did repress us and we would quite like to just not have to deal with it for a generation or two."

Robertson remembers his exposure to faith fondly. The minister, an elderly man with a sunny disposition, lived across the street with his two sisters, and the week before Christmas each year, he would invite young James and his siblings to the manse. After grilling them about their performance in school and "moral condition," he would give them a box of chocolates to take home. Even today, Robertson says he wouldn't mind a bit more peace and quiet on Sunday and a bit less commercialization at Christmastime. But intellectually, he cannot return to being a believer, and he suspects that's true of many Scots. "I'm very, very grateful that I had that religious upbringing because I think it makes me think about bigger, deeper things that I wouldn't if I hadn't had that," he told me. "But

I'm also grateful for the fact that I've got the intellectual ability to make my own choices and step away from it. That is both a legacy of and a reaction to my religious upbringing."

Shortly after graduating from college, lured by America's postwar prosperity and vitality, my father decided to emigrate to the United States. Scotland was struggling economically, its heavy industries such as steel and shipbuilding no longer needed since the end of the war, and his aunt was already there, living in Long Island City and working as a housecleaner for the family of an attorney. My grandparents planned to follow, according to the immigration documents I found in an old footlocker crammed with papers. In November 1953, he got off an ocean liner in New York, but before his parents could make the trip, his mother died unexpectedly. He couldn't afford to go back for the funeral, and wouldn't return to Scotland to visit for some time. He never returned to the Church of Scotland.

] [

In his seminal work, *A Treatise on Human Nature,* published around 1740, David Hume wrote that belief, which he called "this act of mind," had "never yet been explain'd." That didn't stop him from trying, though he was famously skeptical of Christianity, and nearly three centuries later, the heirs to the Enlightenment are still attempting to understand why human beings believe so strongly in things they can neither see nor prove. As I write this, researchers from fourteen of the top universities in the world are at work on a three-year, $3.8 million project to test theories from fields as diverse as evolutionary biology, anthropology, cognitive psychology, even economics: Is faith a by-product of natural selection? A tool to encourage group cohesiveness? A cultural virus preying on unwary minds? Surely standing out in the annals of grant writing for both its brevity and its sheer ambition, their project is named simply "Explaining Religion."

Once, the scientific community steered clear of tackling such mysteries. Conventional wisdom said they were inappropriate, irrelevant, and probably a big waste of time. The realms of reason and religion were separate, distinct, and never the twain should meet. But that changed in the last decade as researchers, emboldened by advancements in technology, began to claim discovery of evidence that would expand our understanding of belief. We got the "God gene," which supposedly predisposed some humans to trust in a higher power; the "God spot," an area of the brain that was purportedly activated during religious experiences; and the "God helmet," a device that some wearers said produced feelings of transcendence and euphoria akin to communing with some cosmic force. Cute names not-withstanding—can the "God pod" be far behind?—none of these alleged breakthroughs held up for long: The gene turned out to be mostly hype, the spot turned out to be just one of several, and at least one skeptic who wore the helmet, über-atheist Richard Dawkins, said he didn't feel a thing. When I called Todd Murphy, the developer of a consumer version of the technology called the Shakti helmet, he told me that he was trying to downplay the device's potential to produce religious experience because it seemed to happen only in limited circumstances. Instead of transcendence, his marketing was emphasizing Shakti's ability to produce "mood enhancement."

Invariably, though, research like this is reported in the media as proof that we are "hardwired for faith," as if our minds are no more complex than a cable TV box (the neon-hued MRIs the scientists produce are but the schematics). And yet it's obvious from the fact that the world's many belief systems have a lot in common that human nature has played a big role in shaping them. Even extreme ideas like spirit possession seem to link millions of people, from indigenous tribes of the Amazon to the Pentecostals of the Bible Belt. This "universal religious repertoire," as it has been called, reinforces suspicions that faith in things unseen is a perfectly natural part of being human, whether as the result of the innate chemistry of our brains or adaptations we have made along the evolutionary road. One of the young stars in this line of work is Oxford researcher Justin Barrett, a thirty-nine-year-old experimental psychologist from Southern California. Barrett's Evangelical faith—before taking his current job, he spent two years helping his wife direct a chapter of Young Life, the Christian group for teens—stands out in psychology, which was once known as the most secular of all the academic disciplines, and it spurred him to want to study the psychology of religion despite its being seen as a dead end for his career. "As a doctoral student, I was reminded that this was a bad idea," he told me. Barrett has made out all right, though, attracting nearly $5 million in grants to fund his research into the "cognitive science of religion," a term he himself is credited with coining.

A key precept of Barrett's work is the notion that religious beliefs are completely natural given the mental tools we all are born with or develop from an early age. One of these tools, which Barrett calls the "hypersensitive agency detection device," is the human tendency to ascribe the cause of events to unseen people or animals. Evolutionary theorists have suggested that this tendency dates to primitive times, when humans had to assume that every sound they heard outside their caves, for instance, was a threat to their safety. If they didn't, if they instead assumed it was nothing instead of something, they risked death. Thus the tendency to detect what psychologists refer to as "agency," even erroneously, was necessary for survival. In experiments, Barrett showed how up to the age of three, children assume that all agents, whether a parent or God, have god-like powers, such as knowing without looking that a box with a picture of crackers on the front actually contains rocks. By age five, children know that humans don't have such powers but still ascribe them to gods. Another tool, known as theory of mind, causes us to assume that the mind of another human works the same way as ours does, but that tendency also allows us to ascribe mental properties to nonhumans, which we continue to do through adulthood, Barrett says. Put these two tools together and it's easy for someone to ascribe agency to supernatural beings. In fact, our minds are tuned to believe in them, and they endure long after childhood is over.

Yet the idea that religion is a natural human tendency causes problems for us nonbelievers. On the one hand, it seems to confirm the idea that believers' minds have been playing tricks on them for a very long time. On the other hand, it suggests that we are the deviant ones, the ones who are going out of our way to work against human nature. *And here I thought we were the slackers.* In fact, the assumption is that there are very few so-called nonbelievers who don't unwittingly still act as if they believe in the supernatural. Barrett argues that there are special conditions that help humans bypass or override the ingrained human tendencies to believe. If we live in a city instead of the country and thus have little contact with nature, we might have no occasion to detect agency that we can't attribute to human action or invention, since we already know why the streetlights change and the cars drive and the elevators go up and down. Similarly, if we don't have to worry about survival, such as where our next meal will come from because we buy food from the grocery store rather than hunting for it or farming it, we might have less cause to put our trust in a supernatural being. If we are affluent, we might have the time to think deeply about whether our supernatural explanations for life are actually plausible, and in certain institutions, universities especially, biases against such explanations will reinforce that.

And just as with religion, the behaviors that arise from these conditions are self-reinforcing. Citing behavioral psychology, Barrett told me that if we act like we don't put much faith in God—don't go to church or pray regularly, for instance—we are less likely to believe in God in the first place. Religion is natural, in part, because we make it that way, and the same goes for irreligion. The French philosopher Blaise Pascal famously argued that the consequences if one is wrong about the existence of God are much worse for the nonbeliever than the believer, so the rational choice was belief. In *The Testament of Gideon*

Mack, the protagonist dismisses the idea as silly, since it's preposterous to think that God wouldn't spot an atheist who is merely hedging his bets. But according to Barrett, the intended recipient of this advice was not nonbelievers but believers who needed extra inspiration to bolster their faith. "Pascal was way ahead of his time psychologically," he told me. "He was telling people, if your belief flags, you should act as if you do believe and then you will believe more. If this dynamic is right, then many different personal environmental conditions that prompt one sort of behavior over others can set one person up for belief or unbelief as compared with another."

I pointed out to Barrett that these unusual conditions for atheism that he describes are the very same ones that are assumed by the secularization theory—urbanization, industrialization, postindustrialization, and affluence. Did that mean he thinks atheism will become more common in the future, as many nonbelievers do? "While my account may predict that, it also predicts that it's more fragile, so that bigger changes in environment actually make it disappear again, make it shrink and become more isolated," he said. Because atheism requires extra effort, in essence, it is more susceptible to change than belief, as the reappearance of organized religion in the former Soviet Union and China seems to show.

The cognitive science of religion did a pretty good job

of explaining the absence of faith in my modern, urban, affluent context. Those conditions, coupled with growing up in a family that didn't behave like we believed, in an environment where belief in God was practically taboo, had aided me in overriding my mind's default state, which, being human, was strongly inclined to faith. Barrett's theories also explained why my children had picked up rudimentary religious beliefs so effortlessly. At their young age, it was only natural for them to ascribe agency to unseen beings and assume that the minds of those unseen beings worked the same way theirs did. That made the notion of a supernatural realm seem perfectly reasonable to them, and it would for some time. But knowing that didn't make answering their questions any easier.

[*four*]

HOLY CITY

Go back in almost any unchurched person's family and within a few generations, you'll find ancestors for whom religion was the unwavering focus of life. On a muggy summer morning, I drove southeast on Interstate 95 toward the town of Falcon, North Carolina, population 342, in search of mine. As I left the Raleigh suburbs behind, the superhighway that runs from Maine to Miami shrunk to just two lanes of bumpy concrete divided by a dented gray guardrail. Only a thin veil of lanky pines, looking no steadier than candles on a birthday cake, shielded the low-lying tobacco and cotton fields from the roar of the traffic. It was early, and I would have given a kidney to see a Starbucks, but all I passed was an occasional aged billboard, obscured by the overgrown vegetation, advertising a "24-hour adult café" or some other odd local business.

At State Highway 82, I exited, drove the mile and a half into town, and parked my car on a side street. Gray-haired women were checking themselves in their rearview mirrors and balding men were pulling themselves out of their big sedans. I crossed the lawn to a small white clapboard church set far back from the lazy main drag and shaded by four pine sentries in a square. A sign marked it as the birthplace of the Pentecostal Holiness Church. Inside, three sections of shiny pews, long ago stained the color of strong coffee, were filling up; the only light shone through the tall windows on each side. After taking a seat in the back, I saw a small, well-dressed woman stand up to speak. In the middle of her announcements, a string of nonsensical words rolled smoothly off her tongue—shamabala-la-la-ooh! Not pausing, she finished her sentence as if nothing had happened and sat back down. The Thursday-morning service at Falcon's 108th Annual Camp Meeting had not yet begun, and they were already speaking in tongues.

I glanced at the back wall, behind the lectern and two high-backed chairs, where the lone decoration was a smallish portrait in dark oils hanging at eye level. Staring down from it, their faces pleasant yet serious and determined, were my great-grandparents.

There's an old story about my great-grandfather Julius Culbreth that as a young man he lit cigars with dollar bills to flaunt his family's wealth. It's almost certainly apocryphal. His father owned a general store and a turpentine still and about a thousand acres of land in eastern North Carolina. But the Culbreths were rich merely by the standards of country people in the South during Reconstruction, which is to say, not really, and certainly not enough to waste a greenback showing off for your friends. Julius, the oldest of seven, was energetic and articulate, and though he had the equivalent of just a high school or junior college education, he didn't lack for confidence. In a photo of him and his siblings taken in front of their family's farmhouse, he is the only one not standing in the yard looking soberly at the camera. Instead, he's stretched out on his side on the roof of the front porch, a sly smile visible even at a distance. At twenty-two, he married the woman who had been his music teacher, Venie Bizzell, and one day they were visiting his father's store when the clerk, having just secured a mail route through their rural community, asked him to suggest a name for it, since the one they had been using, Starling's Bridge, was already taken. "Name it Falcon," he said, eyeing a box of pens on the counter with the same name, which is what they did. That story is so elemental to my great-grandfather's legacy that it was part of the eulogy given at his daughter's funeral a century later.

With his intellect and ambition, Julius could have become a lawyer or a businessman or even a minor politician. But his fate changed for good when he was barely twenty-three. His father—who during the Civil War had survived six months in the Elmira, New York, prison camp known as "Hellmira" because so many Confederates there died from disease, hunger, or exposure to bitter cold—contracted pneumonia after undergoing surgery to relieve a nasal condition and died. Six days later, his mother, who at age forty-two had just given birth for the tenth time, succumbed to her grief at losing her husband and died, too. Their newborn son perished four days after that. Suddenly, shockingly, in less than a fortnight, Julius had lost three family members. He and Venie were now responsible for his siblings and his father's estate, including a business that would begin to lose money under their management, to say nothing of a baby of their own born in the midst of all that death. According to an old unpublished obituary for Venie, they "felt a desperate need for Providential guidance, something outside themselves." They found it in the raucous religious experience of a Holiness tent revival.

In the late nineteenth century, Methodism was America's dominant faith, and the Culbreths, having sent many of their sons into the ministry over the years, were strong Methodists. But not a few Methodists had begun to feel that their churches had become too worldly and permissive and that what was needed was a return to the pursuit of the purity taught by the faith's founder, John Wesley. The Holiness movement, as it was known, had come out of northern churches, where "perfectionism" had been preached since the 1840s. Followers called for the revival of "sanctification," a second work of grace subsequent to being saved that would cleanse a Christian's heart for good, according to Wesley's teachings. After the Civil War, this call for reform traveled south and found converts ready to live free of sin as saints on earth. By the 1890s, this movement that had started from within the Methodist Church began to advocate for outright abandonment of the denomination. The sentiment was stirred at electrifying rallies where preachers chastised mainline churches for allowing their congregations to backslide into all manner of sin. They exhorted worshippers to turn against drinking, dancing, socializing, and smoking and cast off their materialism for a simpler way of life until Jesus' imminent return. In the Evangelical tradition that had spread Methodism across the South, the revivals were explosive and emotional affairs during which worshippers cried and yelled and fell to the ground in fits of shakes. Hence the nickname "Holy Rollers."

In the spring of 1896, the Reverend A. B. Crumpler, who would become known as the father of the Holiness movement in North Carolina, brought this message to the town of Dunn, where my great-grandparents lived at the time. They decided to go to find out what all the fuss was about. As far as I know, they never wrote about what they saw that night. But Florence Goff, an evangelist who grew up in Dunn, described it in her memoir:

> Some said the preacher had powder and scattered on the folks and that they fell like dead men and lay for hours. They fell, it was true, but it was by the mighty power of God. Oh! that Dunn meeting; never will be forgotten. Never was one like it before, nor hasn't been since in this country. Brother Crumpler brought several workers with him, men and women filled with the Holy Ghost. They could sing, shout, preach, or pray—the whole band, girls and boys, men and women. They soon had the town and surrounding country in a stir. Brother Crumpler could be heard preaching on a still night fully two miles, and the Lord was on him so people could not stand it. They screamed and prayed all over town, all up and down the road and all around the whole country.

When Crumpler called worshippers to the altar, my great-grandfather fell in behind my great-grandmother as she made her way to the front. There, they accepted this strange new blessing from the Reverend Crumpler. Afterward, they put her wedding ring in the offering plus a small diamond they had received as a gift when their daughter was born. They had reached a turning point in their young lives. Fifty-six years later, when Julius died, his body was entombed next to Venie's in a mausoleum, on top of which is etched a time line of their life. The very first date is 1896, followed by the words, "Born again, Sanctified wholly, Dedicated for service."

] [

Okay, confession time: I have always had a hard time believing in things that I can't see. I've never been all that interested in ghosts or apparitions or superstitions. I am, in the words of my high school history teacher, a linear thinker. Not like the classmate of mine who could decipher the outlandish Joan Miró painting in our tenth-grade world history textbook. Not like my brother, who spent his spare time teaching himself about UFOs, the Loch Ness monster, and Dungeons & Dragons. My tastes ran to playing with my Legos and watching *Dallas*. When I was a teenager, my mother tried to get me to read *Drawing on the Right Side of the Brain*. Little did she know I had been born with two left lobes. To this day, I can't attest to any experiences I would describe as otherworldly or mystical or even all that spiritual. I have given an above-average amount of time to silent reflection, communing with nature, enjoying art and literature, but none of it has induced feelings that I recognized as transcendence. I even tried dropping acid at a Grateful Dead concert one summer during college. All that induced was anxiety and paranoia, feelings I was already quite familiar with from real life. In the words of my friend Cotton, I don't need the supernatural. The natural is super enough for me.

Some of the best times Cristina and I had enjoyed as a couple had been in the outdoors: the mountain bike ride during graduate school when we had our first long talk, canoeing the Green River down the eastern edge of Utah after graduation, camping in West Texas and Colorado after getting married. So to celebrate our tenth anniversary, we arranged to leave the children with her sister and mother in Texas and spend a glorious week tramping through Yosemite National Park by ourselves. The Scottish naturalist John Muir, who persuaded Teddy Roosevelt to designate the Sierra wilderness America's first national park, likened his early time there to "feasting at the Lord's mountain house," and even now, packed with tourists and school groups, Yosemite remains a gracious and bountiful host. On the second-to-last day of the trip, we walked amid the giant sequoias in the Mariposa Grove, marveling at their serene, surreal dominion over everything else around them. This cluster of trees, each hundreds of feet of muscular trunk and high canopy, is one of the park's top attractions, and as we followed the path that zigzags through them, we were surrounded by fellow gawkers. I wondered how many of the Christians among us were thinking about God as they craned their necks to witness these towering natural miracles. An NFL running back crosses the goal line in a preseason scrimmage and immediately signals his thanks to the Almighty above, but how often does anyone do the same upon witnessing something this magnificent? How many Christians even knew this existed? I smugly asked myself. Didn't these enormous redwoods represent the ultimate in divine artistry and might? Couldn't one see the very breath of the divine in their beauty? What could top this as a spiritual experience? I stopped to let Cristina catch up to me.

—If there were a church at the end of this trail, I'd join it right now.

She gave me a look that said she wasn't exactly buying my self-righteous declaration, and then went back to looking up at the trees and down at the heavy oblong cones they deposited on the ground. Anyway, there *is* a church in Yosemite, a quaint little wood-sided chapel in a meadow below the breathtaking Half Dome. We had passed by it on a walk earlier in the week, snapped a digital photo, and then moved on.

On the airplane back home, I sat in a row of three with a pastor and his wife from a small town in Virginia who were returning from a conference. After attempting to describe what I had seen in the Mariposa Grove, I asked if they had ever been to Yosemite.

—Is that where Yogi Bear lives?

—No, that's *Jellystone.*

] [

I had been fascinated by my great-grandfather's life since I was a child, perhaps because my middle name is Culbreth, but I had been to the place where he spent most of his adult life, the place that bore his imprint more than anyone else's, only a handful of times. Once, I accompanied my mother to Falcon for a dedication ceremony for a stone marker honoring Julius. Other than her, I was the youngest person there by half a century. Upon meeting me, more than one elderly lady told me I resembled him. "I can see the favor," was how they put it. Hard not to like that.

Officiating at the morning service the day I visited Camp Meeting was the Reverend Jimmy Whitfield, the assistant bishop for the state body of the International Pentecostal Holiness Church. The little tabernacle was the place where in 1911 the Pentecostal Holiness Church and the Fire-Baptized Holiness Church merged, forming what's now the IPHC. Julius had built it some years before, using trees felled in a tornado and giving it eight sides to mimic the shape of the tent where he and Venie had been sanctified. He thought the community needed a place for prayer meetings. Today locals call it "the Octagon," softening the last syllable so that it rhymes with "Oregon."

Tall and slim, Whitfield had an easygoing manner about him that ruled out the fiery revivalist preaching I had been expecting. After saying a few words, he asked an older gentleman in the back to lead the church in prayer. The man began and gradually everyone joined in, but they were not following in a prayer book or a bulletin or even praying in unison. Instead, each said his or her own prayer. The result was the aural equivalent of a thick soup, with "Praise Jesus" and "Please God" and "Thank you, Lord" and who knows what else all blending together. Some were despairing, others joyful, but most were soft, monotone, and repetitive, with only the occasional shout or cry rising above the din. A few minutes later, when Whitfield asked for a song, a man in the front row went to the old black upright in the corner, sat down, and began stamping the floor with his foot in time with a rollicking old-fashioned hymn. Almost immediately commenced singing, dancing, hand-clapping, and arm-raising. There were no hymnals and no need for them because everyone knew the words except for me. I felt myself wishing that weren't true, wishing I could join in this suddenly upbeat worship. It was like being at a party where everyone else was dancing and wishing you knew how or had the courage to try to learn. I didn't care that I was out of place; I felt I was missing out. Imagine standing mute and motionless in the middle of a gospel choir. I was in the midst of world-class worshippers, as devout and enrapt as any band of faithful could be, and all I could do was watch. When the congregation was fully revved, the pianist began repeating verses at will until it was time to sit down and listen to a sermon, and I imagined that anybody there would have been happy to get up and give it, so perfectly in tune with one another these believers were.

After the service, as I walked around back to the adjacent restrooms, a man I had seen inside reached the door at the same time as I did. During the hymn, he was the one in the front row pumping his outstretched arms into the air like a coach cheering his star player from the sidelines. He was middle-aged and wore a collarless brown golf shirt and matching slacks and a cell phone holstered at his hip. We walked in together and took adjoining urinals. He waited a moment and then, without turning his head, asked if I had heard the sermon, which was given by a Marine chaplain who counseled vets returning from Iraq and Afghanistan with posttraumatic stress disorder. Afterward, Whitfield had asked worshippers to come forward and encircle their guest speaker in a "prayer of protection," to support his work. Both men had wept openly, and neither for the first time that morning.

—Did you hear what the man had to say? my interlocutor asked over the short partition dividing us.

—Yes.

—Were you in the military?

—Beg your pardon?

—Were you ever in the service?

—No. But I certainly admire the courage it takes.

—I came back from Vietnam, and I was a mess. What the man was saying is true. Seventeen years I had nightmares. Then I accepted Jesus. Never had another one.

He zipped up and turned to the double sink to wash his hands, slip a comb out of his back pocket and run it through his hair, and then returned to his monologue.

—Some of my buddies who were over there still can't deal with it. They refuse to go to Jesus, that's why. It's the only way.

I didn't know how to respond other than to sputter a lame acknowledgment that he must be right. I realized that I had just been evangelized. In the bathroom. *First time for everything*, my father would have said.

The pictures of the early Camp Meetings invariably showed a sea of worshippers flooding the little town of Falcon. In 1900, a missionary passing through town had mentioned to my great-grandfather that he had a large revival tent and fifty surplus tepees from the Spanish-American War and was interested in holding an event in the style of the frontier revivals of the Second Great Awakening, which had done so much to multiply the Methodist ranks. Julius, it turned out, had been thinking along the same lines, and he offered property inherited from his parents as the site. That August, a large crowd of Holiness enthusiasts showed up for ten days of prayer and preaching and nights lit by the moon and five-foot-high lightwood bonfires. In the years after, the annual event attracted crowds in the thousands, and was followed by my great-grandfather's opening a Holiness school and an orphanage. Transplants came to live in a community free of the moral turpitude of the day, speaking of Falcon as a "holy city." They held themselves to Holiness standards, which meant dressing simply and conservatively (one minister once said he'd rather have a rattlesnake around his neck than wear a tie, and some considered it a sin), eschewing alcohol and Coca-Cola, and avoiding dance halls and movie theaters, of which there were none in Falcon anyway. Even tobacco, the king crop of the state, was forbidden, thanks to the resolution Julius introduced at the national conference to ban members from growing, selling, or using it. Mainline churchgoers derided Holiness believers as low-class, uneducated bumpkins, which, as often happens with persecution, only served to embolden them to fulfill what they saw as their calling.

There was much less energy in the modern Camp Meeting, though, which seemed fitting for a speck of a town that today has neither a restaurant nor a single retail business. The people who had come for the daytime activities were mostly ministers and church officials and retirees. Lunch was served to a half-empty room. As I ate barbecue and drank sweet tea, a jovial forty-eight-year-old pastor named Oris Hubbard strode up and shook my hand. I invited him to sit down. It would turn out that Oris and I could trace our ancestors back to the same hardy Scottish settler who had arrived in these parts in the mid–eighteenth century. The difference was that Oris's family was still here. He had grown up in Falcon, and his father still lived in the same house, the one where his mother once operated the town post office out of a little shed in the front yard, the same one my mother would have gone to when asked on a visit to pick up the mail for her grandparents. He grew up in the church and eagerly awaited Camp Meeting each year. After a year studying accounting at the University of North Carolina at Chapel Hill, he transferred to the IPHC affiliated Holmes Bible College, where he met the woman he would marry, Rose. She turned out to be the niece of his childhood pastor, who went on to be the church's national leader.

As a child, Oris had imbibed from the spiritual well my great-grandfather dug here, and he retained an old-timer's affection for the place. He had recently bought a rental property in town, "so I could have my little piece of Falcon," he told me. After lunch, he took me next door to the decrepit low-ceilinged hall where Camp Meetings had been held for eight decades. When the hall opened in 1926, the floor was nothing but wood shavings, and the open windows were covered with only chicken wire. Now, too costly to bring up to code, the hall was slated for demolition. A new building had already gone up, but that one, Oris noted, would never rumble and shake the way this more primitive one had. There were even questions about the future of Camp Meeting. The simple charm of Falcon had once been a beacon for Holiness folk, a symbol of their remove from the carnal temptations of the world. But for much of today's IPHC, the denomination's austere beginnings hold little meaning, the isolation—social, cultural, economic— little attraction. There's a younger generation who want a more modern and inviting style of worship, with cushioned seats instead of hard pews and contemporary Christian songs in place of the old-timey hymns. They don't refer to one another as "Brother," and they find the traditional strictures of Holiness life increasingly anachronistic. Oris thinks of himself as a bridge between these two worlds. On a table outside his office sat a week's supply of Diet Coke, which once would have qualified as contraband, and when his secretary's phone rang, it played the Evangelical anthem "Awesome God." He eats out on Sundays and even takes in a movie occasionally, both of which would have been unthinkable for someone in his position just fifteen years ago. The church's growth is dominated by immigrants from Mexico and Central and South America, and the service that evening would be bilingual, featuring a well-known Latino evangelist from Florida. Oris was expecting a good turnout from congregations in the area. "They show up big," he told me with genuine appreciation. "The face of this church is changing."

] [

I certainly don't need to be an eyewitness to everything I hold true. As an adolescent, I would say, if asked, that I believed in a supreme being, and I think I truly did. Not God necessarily, just some nebulous cosmic force that didn't require much further explanation. More than anything else, I think it was an attempt to deflect a question that made me deeply uncomfortable. Now it's a question I can't seem to escape. We took a family trip recently to see an old friend who was a minister of a congregation on the coast, and on Sunday morning we all went to hear him preach. The church dated to 1830; in back lay an ancient cemetery with gargantuan oaks garbed in heavy robes of brittle gray moss. In the sanctuary, sunlight streamed in through the large windows. We found an empty pew on the left, opened the low door, and slid in. When the organ began to play the processional, we all stood, my son climbing onto the seat to get a better look. We made eye contact and he smiled self-consciously. I leaned in so we could hear each other.

—What's up?

—I wish God was alive.

I fumbled for a lame response, along the lines of "How do you know He's not?" or "Maybe He is," or "Well, some people believe . . ." and he immediately slumped his shoulders and grinned to let me know that was not what he meant.

—I wish God was here.

It has become common for Christians to argue that the complexity of life could only be the handiwork of a divine creator who made the world as it is. But the very same people who make this argument are quick to tell us not to expect to ever see with much clarity the contours of the intelligent designer's divinity. For every phenomenon that they chalk up to His intervention—the wonder of human reproduction, for example—there's another— the heartbreak of bearing a child with autism or Down syndrome—that is said to be beyond our keenest insight. "The Lord works in mysterious ways" and "It's God's will"

and "Ours is not to reason why, ours but to do and die."
For someone trained to think critically and question everything, that wisdom is impossible to accept.

One day, my friend Cotton mentions to me that a friend
of his attends a church and the pastor is a hologram. I do
some research and identify the virtual preacher as Andy
Stanley, head of the 16,000-member North Point Community Church in the suburbs of Atlanta. Each week, his
sermon is recorded for viewing the following week by a
congregation downtown. The $250,000 high-definition
projection system makes it look like he's right there in
the room.

Curious to know more about Stanley, I dig up video of
one of the sermons on the Internet. The title was "Belief
in God: It's Personal," the first of a four-part series, accompanied by slick graphics, aimed at non-Christians.
Now, if there ever was a style of religion that I would go
out of my way to avoid—big, modern, high-tech—this was
it. And yet as I watched him, I couldn't seem to pull myself
away. Perched casually on a stool with a Bible spread out
on the table next to him, he spoke in an affable manner
that is increasingly the norm among mega-church leaders.
He's fifty-one and a father of three, but in an open-collared
shirt and jeans he looked like a much younger man, perhaps one of the suburban professionals who make up a big
part of his congregation. His message, delivered in a gentle,

unassuming tone that he occasionally injected with dead-pan humor, was simple: You probably have valid reasons for not being a Christian. Perhaps, for instance, you just doubt that a loving God would allow all the evil that exists in the world. Or perhaps you feel like you'd be betraying parents or grandparents who taught you not to believe. Well, he said, everyone has questions about the existence and nature of God, even the most devout believers. But the need to answer those questions is nothing compared with the need to know God. When you become a Christian, he argued, the doubts don't go away, you haven't squelched them, they just get smaller. In guiding his audience through this concept, Stanley went out of his way to affirm the validity of whatever concerns they might have about Christianity. But then he told them, in effect, to table those doubts for the time being. Don't forget them, just put them aside and perhaps they will shrink. "[God] wants to know you more than He wants you to have the answers to all of your questions," he said. "That's the bottom line."

Toward the end of the thirty-five-minute sermon, Stanley asked the worshippers to say a simple prayer during the next week telling God that you want to know Him more than you want to have answers to your questions. It didn't matter if you believed or not. "If there's no God, you're just talking to the air," Stanley said, and it occurred to me on hearing this that he was right. What did anyone have to lose? I imagined what I might look like saying a quiet prayer into the rearview mirror of my car, as he suggested. Could it really be that easy? Maybe pushing aside my doubts was the only way, I thought. Maybe I couldn't intellectualize my way into belief. Maybe faith had to trump all else. The whole idea gave me a nervous feeling low in my stomach like the kind I would get as a kid if I was trying to summon the courage to speak in front of a crowd of people or jump off the high diving board. I didn't actually think there was anything on the other side of that feeling. But I didn't really want to find out if there was.

It was like this dream I had. Not one of my usual nightmares, but a short one, an interlude between full-length features. I was in a dim, windowless weight room like the one at which I worked during college, checking IDs and sweeping up after the jocks were finished with their workouts. Lying down underneath a bar spooled with iron plates, I lifted it off its resting spot, let it drop slowly toward my chest, and then pushed it back up until my arms had straightened. My second bench press was more difficult, and my forearms began to quiver. Part of the way into the third, they collapsed, my elbows and hands dropping toward the floor like an elevator with its cable cut, until the bar was literally doing little bunny hops on my chest. I panicked because there was no spotter to lift it off me, no one else even in the room. And then, without warning, the weights flew into the air and disappeared, and I heard a distant voice say, "I am your savior." I woke immediately, my heart racing as if I were still trapped under all that weight, my stomach electrified by anxiety. It was the same feeling I had after listening to Andy Stanley and I couldn't decide if it was fear or embarrassment, but I didn't want to tell anyone about this dream. Was this providential guidance like what Julius and Venie had experienced? Was it a joke, my subconscious mocking my sudden interest in spirituality? Was it for real, and if yes, why had I been chosen for the corniest revelation ever? That night, I told Cristina.

—How do you know it wasn't the Buddha talking to you?

—Good point.

I laughed because I knew she was right. The choice between belief and nonbelief just couldn't be that cut-and-dried. I was tempted to give in, accept something that I didn't really believe could be true, even just for a moment. But I knew my mind wasn't ever going to allow it. The way to my heart still went through my brain. Andy Stanley had made it clear that shoving my doubts to the side was a point of no return, and I wasn't ready for that.

] [

Despite his success, none of Julius's six siblings ever followed him in leaving the Methodist Church. They stayed in Falcon, helping out with Camp Meetings and church services, but quietly some complained that the Holiness transplants treated them as if they were spiritually inferior. All three of his and Venie's children—my grandmother, Ruth, and her two sisters, Merle and Daisy—left Falcon behind once they could leave home. The restrictions of Holiness living and the provinciality of life in the "Holy City" were simply too bleak, too confining. They resented having to compete with the orphans for their father's attention, and they resented the burden their pious and hardworking mother shouldered to support him in all of his endeavors. Later, they resented that he gave his entire life's work—the tabernacle, the Camp Meeting, the orphanage—to the IPHC, leaving them to pay his life insurance premiums in his final years so they would have an inheritance. Of his three daughters, two became pregnant out of wedlock, and only one stayed in the denomination he had helped create.

Indeed, my family didn't like to admit it, but our relationship with my great-grandfather's legacy was fraught with contradiction. He had achieved a measure of import and influence in the world that his descendants revered.

And yet we had largely rejected the manner in which he had achieved it: his radical conversion, his unwavering devotion to his faith, his moralistic pursuit of perfection, and his open embrace of a simple life serving the less fortunate. After one visit to Falcon, my parents grouched that the furnishings had been upgraded (my father referred to them as "plush") as they made their way back to the comfort of the big city. We rejected the notion that Julius might have spoken in tongues, even though, according to a collection of profiles of IPHC leaders, "it is very unlikely that he would have been elected to the positions of high honor" had he not.

At one of the events at the Camp Meeting I attended, when the people in the audience had learned that Julius Culbreth's great-grandson was in their midst, they had broken out in applause. *Applause?* I thought. *For what? If only they knew how little of his belief came with me.* Driving around Falcon, it was hard not to feel like a tourist who had no right to do anything but look quietly. Here were all these monuments to my great-grandfather's religious faith, and they belonged to the people who shared it, not the people who shared merely his name. There was only one Culbreth left in Falcon, an elderly, childless cousin of my grandmother's named Katherine but nicknamed "Kitten" because of her fondness for cats. Hearing that, I thought: This is what secularization looks like. A town left behind. My mother's cousin, a labor lawyer in Washington, told me that when he stops in Falcon on the way home from the beach each summer, he drops a check off at the orphanage perhaps to assuage mild guilt about his disconnection from our ancestral home. The last time he did so, the director asked if he would play the role of Julius in a performance to mark the orphanage's hundredth anniversary, perhaps not aware that this cousin is an observant Jew.

I thought about my mother, who had nagged us not to forget our great-grandfather's accomplishments. When one of the houses Julius and Venie had lived in was being torn down, she had rushed to Falcon to grab newel posts and French doors with paint falling off in thick chips and a rotting pine mantelpiece that now hangs above the fireplace in my house. His faith was as much a world away for her as it was for me. But his ethic—diligence, responsibility, leadership, kindness, compassion, and generosity—was the stuff that made a person great. He dedicated his life to something bigger than himself, giving everything he had to helping others. Knowing that had taught us the nobility of a life devoted to a higher purpose, perhaps even a religious one. Perhaps that was why I had an affinity for people, particularly men, who could talk about their faith. Perhaps that's why I felt my family should go to church. Perhaps that was why I didn't steer my children away from believing in God. I couldn't rule out the possibility that inspiration of the magnitude that had struck Julius might one day find them.

In the afternoon, while most of the Camp Meeting attendees were resting, I made a visit to the small cemetery behind Antioch Baptist Church. Julius's parents had donated the land the church sat on, even though they were never members, and, with their infant son, were the first people to be buried there. The wind blew an afternoon storm in from the east as I knelt in front of the headstone marking the grave of Julius's father. Above me, a magnolia stood, its limbs stretched out protectively like the worshippers surrounding the weeping chaplain that morning, the only shade on an oppressively humid day. Under my feet were patchy grass and weeds that formed an unruly ground cover with the moss and sand. "The heart's keen anguish only those can tell who've bid the dearest and best farewell," the epitaph read. My mother had quoted it in a eulogy for her mother that she wrote but never gave. The wind blustered again, then stilled, then whipped up once more. Broken adornments lay propped against other headstones, and a few plots bore sadly weathered plastic bouquets. The cemetery was no less alive than any other place in this slumbering little town, each headstone bearing testament to the resilience of death, of remembrance, of cemeteries. Falcon never was much of a "holy city," not really much more than a company town (though it would have prospered more if the church had accepted my great-grandfather's offer to locate its college there). But you would have had to believe it was to ever want to spend much time here. You would have to believe in either the holiness of realizing God's kingdom on earth or the holiness of love, of family, of the undying pain of those of us "who bid the dearest and best farewell." Julius and Venie had chosen the former and were buried a mile or so away at a cemetery he established so that church members would have a final resting place. For my mother, their granddaughter, it was the latter, and that was why I was here, bent at the knees and brushing off the dirt that caked around the bottoms of these markers.

] [

The new home of Camp Meeting services, the two-year-old Julius A. Culbreth Memorial Auditorium, was a cavernous multipurpose room with a high-end sound system and large video screens on the wall. I got there early and watched as a large crowd of Hispanic men, women, and children filed in and found seats, some of them edging by older Anglo couples who were already seated. Soon, the state body's Hispanic leader was switching between Spanish and English to rev up the crowd. "Did you bring the praise with you?" he asked excitedly. "*¡Diga Aleluya! ¡Diga Aleluya!*" Then the service began with a procession of teenagers carrying the flags of the different countries represented in their churches to the tinny sound of recorded music. Afterward the Reverend Whitfield came to the lectern. "I don't know what language they speak in heaven," he said in his good-natured drawl, "but the Hispanic language sure is a pretty one." A century ago, the Holiness movement had distinguished itself by welcoming all races. The man who introduced speaking in tongues to North Carolina had learned it worshipping with African-Americans in Los Angeles, and the middle name Julius gave to my great-aunt Daisy was that of an evangelist well known for his outreach to former slaves. That openness ended by the early 1920s with Jim Crow, though, and it wasn't until near the end of the twentieth century that the IPHC stood up again for racial harmony. However awkward and opportunistic, this attempt at bridging two cultures struck me as kind of remarkable.

A bit later, after some praying and singing, came the altar call, and in ones and twos people got up out of their seats and walked to the front of the stage. Several pastors stood waiting to grab these supplicants by the shoulders and bring them in close and pray for God to have mercy on them. The pastors had with them special oil with which to anoint those in need of healing, just as Julius had hoped Oral Roberts would do for him. Some of the worshippers wept, and a few shook out of grief or joy, I didn't know which. Once again, I felt drawn to participate, and the nervousness returned to my gut. I wanted to know what was going on up there. I wanted a taste of whatever it was they were serving up. But I also knew it would be wrong. To walk up there simply out of curiosity and feign interest in something I didn't think was real . . . I couldn't do that in a building named for my great-grandfather.

There's another story about Julius my uncle Dave told me recently, which I like to think is true. "When Grandpa was in the hospital and dying of uremic poisoning, Mother and Daddy went to visit him," Dave told me as we sat at the table in his kitchen. "Daddy, with his usual diplomacy, said, 'Well, Mr. Culbreth, how do you feel about your religious beliefs now?' And Grandpa said, 'It's hard. It's hard. Doubt is easy.'"

[*five*]

BACHELOR 'TIL THE RAPTURE

I came back from my visit to Falcon with the prayers of Pentecostals playing in an endless loop in my head. Occasionally one would spill out. "Praise Jesus," I would blurt out softly as I put away a dish. "Thank you, Lord," I muttered as I got into bed. I didn't mean it, obviously. I thought it was funny. Cristina disagreed and politely told me to stop. Was she worried that I might have returned from Camp Meeting a changed man—saved, sanctified, and dedicated for service? Funny, for every inch that my mind was opening to Christianity, hers threatened to close just as much. Speaking in tongues? Prayer of protection? Testifying in the toilet? These people are clearly nuts, I sensed her wanting to tell me. I hadn't even mentioned that the early tongues-speakers thought they were speaking a foreign language, so they sent missionaries to far-off lands where they thought they would be understood, only to be greeted by blank stares. I couldn't necessarily disagree with my wife. Maybe they were nuts. But they were my people, too.

] [

For most of my childhood, my family lived in a split-level house. The split-level was a marvel of postwar American architecture. In the same amount of space found in your average one-story ranch, a split-level offered three separate floors, each its own private plain of existence to which one could retreat for work or play, so while the children were doing their homework upstairs in their bedrooms, mom could be cooking dinner in the kitchen on the middle level while dad reclined in front of the news in the down-stairs den. This describes approximately what was happening one evening during eighth grade when I ventured out of my room to get an ETA on supper. Trotting down the half-flight of stairs that led from the top to the middle level, I passed the longer flight leading to the bottom level and breezed into the kitchen. My mother was alone, her back to me as she faced the beige electric stove, but I could see that something was wrong. Dinnertime was al-ways something of a witching hour—the stress of my father's quest for tenure, the loneliness of my mother's standard-issue domestic entrapment, and the adolescent anxieties gripping my older brother and me all stewed together, needing little encouragement to reach a high rolling boil. Then: yelling, door slamming, door opening, stomping up and down stairs, and backing the car quickly out of the driveway for dramatic effect. My brother and my mother were the most common combatants, but the split-level had seen all of us lose our grip at one time or another. This time, though, I didn't hear any fighting; I had only the vague feeling that some serious and perhaps somewhat heated conversation had just ended before I walked in. Seeing me, my mother looked up and then back to the stove without interrupting her stirring, her face a blend of shock and sadness. I asked what was wrong, and in a clipped, muted tone that in other families would be reserved to discuss drug abuse or divorce or white-collar crime, she told me.

—Your brother just informed us that he is now a Christian.

What the son wishes to forget, the grandson wishes to remember.

] [

As a child, my brother showed a precocious intellect. He also had an intensity about him inherited from Mama that led the two of them into frequent fights. By his teen years, he had abandoned conventional little-boy interests for more specialized ones: Egyptology, the Mongols, the viola. He subscribed to *OMNI* magazine (and insisted that I wash my hands thoroughly before touching an issue). He would be the first to acknowledge that even at a young age there was a self-seriousness to his pursuits that sometimes lapsed into perfectionism, but there was much more to him than that. He was kind and compassionate and often outrageously funny. He was also an atheist. He had discussed this with my parents, with whom he shared a deep connection due to their shared intellect, and I assume they appreciated that he had come to this position on his own. It probably seemed appropriate that a child growing up in the modern world would have little inclination to take religion seriously.

My brother is the most ethical person I know. Once, I tried to give him a cassette of some music I thought he might like. He refused it on the grounds that in making it I might have violated U.S. copyright law. I've often thought his personal rectitude might be related to having an unusual name: Ewan. He's gone through life with no hope of ever hiding his sins in anonymity, and I think that's steeled him against embarrassments that would crush the rest of us. Ewan is a common Scottish name, but when we were kids, back before offbeat names became chic in the suburbs, it might as well have been Swahili. Most people overreached and called him by the last name of the star center then playing at Georgetown, Patrick Ewing. But when his tenth-grade biology teacher got to his name on her roll, "Ewan Park" came out "Urine Pox," which sounded like a painful condition one might learn about in tenth-grade biology. He somehow laughed it off. Once, he let me tag along with him to a grubby punk-rock dive that was the only nightclub in town where you could hear alternative bands play. As we approached the front door, a guy who looked like a regular was snickering about the conservative way Ewan was dressed. I was immediately ashamed, as much for myself as I was for my brother, but he delivered a quick retort that instantly shut the jerk up, something along the lines of "Gee, I thought this was the kind of place where people didn't care what kind of clothes you wore." We made our way inside, never breaking stride, my insecurity momentarily giving way to pride.

When you have only one sibling, especially an older one, you spend a lot of your time thinking about how the two of you are different. Let me count the ways: My brother is a Jesus-loving, Bible-believing, homeschooling, Evangelical Christian. Of course, that's not all he is: He's also a caring father and husband and an outstanding teacher and a graduate of Swarthmore, Harvard, and Penn. But his faith is at the center of his life, and it has been that way ever since the day he announced it to our bewildered parents. In the intervening twenty-five years, he and I had never spoken at length about his religious beliefs or how it was he had come by them. Was this despite our genuine affection for each other, or because of it? For my part, I think I simply wanted to avoid the strife that nearly destroyed his relationship with our mother and father. He had never hidden his devotion from me, never forgone his silent prayers before every meal or the Christian rock when I rode in his car, and he had never suggested I follow his spiritual path. But he hadn't ever talked openly with me about it, either, and I had never had the courage to ask. (Probably in response to his fieriness, I had from a young age strived for stoicism and equanimity. I loved watching and playing tennis, and adopted as my personal motto the Rudyard Kipling quotation that hangs above the players' entrance to Centre Court at Wimbledon: "If you can meet with triumph and disaster and treat those two impostors just the same.") Perhaps subconsciously, we both recognized that one day we would have only each other. Yet the physical distance between us—he had lived outside of Philadelphia for most of the time since he left for college—meant that our emotional connection frayed easily. On several occasions during the pained deliberations over how best to care for our father in his debilitated condition, it was severed completely, and my instinct at such times was to channel my parents' dismay at how different he was rather than address whatever the real issue was. The day after Daddy died, during an emotional phone conversation, Ewan told me that he had reached out to Jesus in his grief, and he encouraged me to do the same. It was the first time he had ever come close to proselytizing with me, and it made me slightly uncomfortable. But it also touched me. Perhaps with both of our parents now gone, the fearsome consequences of talking openly about what divided us had disappeared, too.

Ewan's conversion, and the reaction it produced, had done more to shape my feelings about religion than anything else in my life. But I had witnessed it only through my parents' jaundiced eyes. I wanted to know what he really believed, and why, and why I didn't, and he was happy to oblige. So not long after that, we started talking, ever so gingerly, sometimes by e-mail, sometimes by phone. One Friday night, when his family was out of the house at dance practice, I asked him how he became a Christian.

] [

Eleventh grade had been a difficult year for Ewan. Two events that spring had rattled him—the suicide of an acquaintance and a friend's paralysis after being hit by a car while on his bicycle—as had his first experience with serious depression. The combination had left him feeling more contemplative than usual. That summer, he attended a program for elite students from across the state. In advanced classes on literature, philosophy, and psychology, he had his first interactions with kids with overtly conservative Christian religious views. Their debates sparked in him an intellectual interest in faith that had been quietly kindling for a year or so, and it intensified as he read *Hamlet* and *Doctor Faustus* and Flannery O'Connor short stories. He also began dating a girl who had recently been saved at a Young Life camp. As they got serious, he began thinking more deeply about the possibility that God existed and the duality of good and evil in the world. He still considered himself an agnostic, but the ideas underlying Christianity had become much more compelling to him and the arguments against them had become less so. His mind was opening: It wasn't the truth, but maybe it wasn't absurd to think about either.

By winter break, he and his girlfriend had split up. But as he explained to me now, the pieces of his spiritual puzzle were coming together. In the days leading up to Christmas he began to sense the presence of God guiding him to faith in a way that he was unable to resist any longer. The effect was thrilling and joyful at the same time; he felt "like a bubble about to burst," he told me. But he realized that his objections had been dealt with, that he believed in it, that he thought what he was feeling was real, and that it was time to behave as if it was. He was a Christian now, and there was no longer any sense in denying it. Alone in his room one night, he dropped to his knees on the carpet and he began to pray. "It was like, 'Oh, my goodness, this is real, and I'm not just playing a game anymore,'" he told me. "It wasn't like a diminution of my normal faculties. It was simply like I suddenly had a new faculty, and my other faculties and it were all there and working together. Or like going from being able to see everything in two dimensions to suddenly seeing everything in three, like I was experiencing a dimension of reality I had never experienced before."

It would be hard to imagine a more perfectly executed teenage rebellion. Being born-again was to our family what stealing a car or getting pregnant or huffing glue in the garage were to most others. This was an assault on our parents' most cherished values so blatant that it was practically comical. *Take that, you lily-livered liberals! You think you're so tolerant? Tolerate this!* Or at least, that's what I had always assumed. But I had been wrong. Ewan told me he had been eager to relay this news, especially to our mother, who he thought would be delighted by it. He thought of her as still being a believer, no matter how lapsed in her commitment, and because of that he had worried that his atheism upset her. Yes, she griped about Jerry Falwell and his ilk, but that was precisely because she thought of herself as a Christian and was offended by the way she saw them abusing that label. "I was going to tell her, and she was going to be overjoyed, almost like the Prodigal come home," he told me.

This revelation stunned me. I thought about the nervous stomach I had been getting when on the brink of some kind of acceptance of the possibility of the divine. In retrospect, it was hard not to feel sympathy for an adolescent who is greeted with that same kind of excitement. But Mama wasn't overjoyed, and neither was our father, and they made no effort to hide it. In their mind, Evangelical Christianity conjured up narrow-minded, anti-intellectual, moralizing buffoons. They were appalled that one of their children would choose to identify with a belief system so at odds with how they had brought him up, and just as he was about to go out into the world on his own. Very little was required to turn them into left-wing Archie Bunkers full of indignation that their firstborn could be caught up in something so foolish. Our proximity to the Evangelical ascendance only made it that much more difficult for my parents to keep quiet. The intellectual conversations they had enjoyed having with their son soon morphed into pitched debates over whose vision of what constituted morality was right. Indeed, they seemed less concerned about the inner workings of my brother's religious faith than the influence it had on his feelings about political and social issues, culture and education. They were stunned at how radically his worldview had changed. For instance, he was now pro-life and believed nonbelievers went to hell. My mother told

Ewan that they'd never be able to relate to him in the same way again, never be able to talk about ideas again, that he had become narrow-minded and might as well have joined the Ku Klux Klan. My father was less direct, comparing his new beliefs to the philosophies of the Khmer Rouge and the Know-Nothing Party. "It was not so much that Evangelicalism was detested," Ewan said. "It wasn't an option. It was the anti-option. It took me a long time to understand I couldn't argue them into thinking this was a great thing."

But argue he did. If Ewan hadn't set out to rile my parents, he had no trouble doing so once they provoked him. If they were so open-minded, why were they responding to him so hysterically? Why did their tolerance turn into cynicism and superiority when it came to people with whom they disagreed? Why wasn't his acceptance of Christian faith a positive development? It was a backhanded attack on the lack of spiritual direction in their own lives. He even brought up Jim Bakker, who was beginning to take heat in the local media for his prosperity gospel and the lavish lifestyle for him and Tammy Faye that it was financing. Mama and Daddy's worldview exalted human possibility and the accomplishments of great thinkers and artists and musicians, yet they seemed to have little sympathy for someone who evinced the most human of failings, whose behavior demonstrated how imperfect humans are and how easy it is for any of us to fall short of being morally good. "People often complain about the smugness of the churches they grew up in," Ewan told me. "This was just my version of it."

] [

Morality is a funny thing. Most people, whether they're religious or not, don't actually stop to consider the unending stream of ethical judgments they make every day that determine how they behave. The big ones—the ones encompassed by the term "basic human decency"—aren't really up for debate. Others we can trace to specific influences: our parents, a memorable teacher, a defining moment. But religion has less of an impact on most people's decision making than you might think. When the Pew Forum on Religion and Public Life asked American adults recently whether they believed there were "absolute standards of right and wrong," solid majorities of both the total population and the nonreligious said yes, 78 percent and 67 percent, respectively. But when the same people were asked what specifically they looked to for guidance when faced with questions concerning right and wrong, only 29 percent chose "religious teachings and beliefs," and more than half said "practical experience and common sense."

And remarkably, only 10 percent of Jews, 22 percent of Catholics, 24 percent of mainline Protestants, and 52 percent of Evangelical Protestants—barely a moral majority—said they consciously sought direction from their faith.

And yet many Christians assume that to be a nonbeliever is to lack a moral foundation. Tim Keller, pastor of Redeemer Presbyterian Church, a conservative Evangelical congregation in New York City, argues that the existence of right and wrong proves that God is real, because only a divine creator could be the source of standards that supersede human wants and needs. Keller's argument isn't so much based on the truth claims of Christianity as it is on the rejection of a human-centered worldview, and he criticizes those who think that to be a Christian is to be morally superior. But the implication is clear either way: No religion, no right and wrong. "If there is no God, then there is no way to say any one action is 'moral' and another 'immoral' but only 'I like this,'" he writes in his 2008 book, *The Reason for God*. "It is dishonest to live as if he is there and yet fail to acknowledge the one who has given you all these gifts."

Whenever I hear someone say that nonreligious people are amoral or relativistic, I invariably think about my mother, a woman whose moral judgments had all the flexibility of a hundred-year-old oak trunk. Because she came of age in the 1950s and never engaged in the libertinism of the decade that followed, she had pretty traditional notions of what constituted the right behavior when it came to things like underage drinking, taking drugs, or premarital sex. But that was low-hanging fruit, and she let us know it frequently. We were to be kind to our fellow human beings and treat everyone fairly and equally. We were to be honest and trustworthy and respectful of our elders. We were to be compassionate, caring, and loving, and turn the other cheek when others were not. We were to challenge ourselves academically and model responsibility and self-control in the classroom. Equal parts holiness and humanist, this code of ethics was never described in religious terms, but it was no less certain in her mind than if it had been divinely sent. It was almost as if she was overcompensating for our family's lack of piety by instilling in us a sense of duty to our fellow human beings that could stand up to anything being preached from a pulpit. A few times, she went so far as to plot our performance on these measures on poster-sized charts, but it wasn't like there was any room for failure. When I was fifteen and got in trouble for my peripheral connection to a prank involving a pornographic movie and my school's closed-circuit television system—*it might have been my idea*—my mother outlined, in a typewritten letter to me, the danger that I might fall short of her expectations:

Please don't assume that good character is something
one is born with, like intelligence or blue eyes; on the
contrary, character grows out of experience in which it
is tested and it requires the same kind of exercise and
self-discipline your mental faculties need if it is to
develop. Making good decisions in your life will not come
automatically to you just because you are at heart a good
and decent person, as I know you are. You must work at
developing your conscience, your sense of what is right
for you to do, and your determination not to allow others
to make decisions for you. It is not too early for you to
spend some time visualizing the kind of person you want
to become by the time you are a high school senior, how
you view yourself and how you want others to think
of you. You should set those goals now so that they will
be in your mind as you make decisions and face
temptations.

It went on for three single-spaced pages. As the firstborn, though, Ewan had it worse. As early as age four or
five, he was already concerned that he might never turn
out to be a good boy. That insecurity stuck with him and,
ironically, would eventually play a major role in his embrace of Christianity. He had wrestled with morality and
questioned why every act of human altruism seemed to
have a rotten core of self-interest. Only through faith in

a transcendent God, he came to believe, could one pursue true goodness. "I realized I would logically never be able to be a moral person if I was the central reference point in the universe. And if there really was no God, then this was not even a possibility and I would be forever caught in a trap of doing good things but for essentially selfish motivations. When I became a Christian, part of what I was realizing was, I couldn't really be the kind of good person I want to be without God."

] [

After a tumultuous spring and summer, my brother went off to college, happy to be free of the blowups at home and excited to pursue his newfound faith in new ways and with new people. Our parents felt no such relief, though. As time went on, their unhappiness with his choices turned to fear about where they would take him. When he came home for the summer, the arguments resumed, but now they were concerned that his personality had changed, that he had become even more determined in his social, political, and religious views, and that his religious life was taking precedence over his academic and family life. When, during his sophomore year, he decided to spend the following summer living with a group of guys in a run-down house in the inner city of Philadelphia, they began to worry that he might have gotten involved in something that was much more dangerous and manipulative.

The house was known as the Zoo, and the idea was for these young Christians from different colleges in the area to nurture their faith, live a simple, communal lifestyle, and minister to the poor in this neighborhood. Ewan took a job driving a truck for a secondhand store during the day. For dinner they ate government cheese and bulk fruits and vegetables. On Friday evenings, they gathered together to sing, pray, and talk. They even pledged to remain single and celibate in order to focus on serving God, calling themselves "Bachelors 'til the Rapture." "We prized radicalness," he told me. "What's more countercultural than to be a college student devoted to singleness?" My parents had a much darker view, though. He was living in an extremely dangerous environment (though they didn't know until later that he had been assaulted by drug dealers). And the Spartan diet made them think that someone might be trying to soften their son up for some sort of indoctrination. Sensory deprivation was a well-established mind-control tactic, and less than a decade after Jonestown, there were plenty of instances they could point to in which it had been used. In retrospect, perhaps their fear was understandable, Ewan admitted. "You just look at my personality type, and I'm totally the type of person who would join a cult."

Throughout this, my brother and I managed to stay civil with each other, at least superficially. After Mama and Daddy made an unannounced visit to campus in a unsuccessful attempt to get him to take time off and return home, I was dispatched, like an envoy to North Korea hoping to discern some channel for diplomacy. On the first day of my visit, he attended a Bible study while I read. Afterward, I asked him how it went, and he told me that he had really felt the Lord's Spirit in the room. I didn't know how to respond. My brother was speaking a foreign language. On Sunday, I accompanied him to church. At the climax of the service, he stood, arms raised in exultation, seemingly transfixed in worship. I stayed seated on the hard pew, my head in my hands. It felt like a betrayal. Not because there was something wrong with what they were doing, but because there was something wrong with him doing it.

As we waited at the airport for my flight to board, I mentioned that I was concerned that I might be left to take care of our parents in their old age. I didn't mention that our parents had found a flyer in his room for missionaries to Mongolia. I think he was confused as to why his seventeen-year-old little brother would be worried about such things, but I was merely mimicking what I was hearing at home. After spending more than a year researching cults, including fundamentalist Christian ones, they were making plans to bring a deprogrammer to Charlotte. A friend offered her house at the lake for the weekend, and my parents paid for Ewan to fly home under the pretense that we would spend a relaxing week together before he had to return for the start of classes. He never considered that it might be a ruse to stage an intervention because he never believed he was in a cult.

It was August and my senior year had just started, but I was allowed to miss a day of school to participate. For two days we sat around a large sectional sofa, playing a surreal game of musical chairs as different friends and family members engaged him in teary conversations. The deprogrammer told Ewan about being trapped in a coercive group in the 1970s in which one of the members had committed suicide, and then he showed a video that showed members of a similar group being mass hypnotized into believing they were members of an orchestra and playing musical instruments that weren't there. But my brother was unmoved. "I was like, 'What does that have to do with me?'" he told me. "For all the wacky things, I knew that I had made a conscious choice to get involved in the Zoo. No one had pressured me, no one had forced me."

My parents could tell they were getting nowhere. On Sunday morning, Ewan woke up early and left the lake house on foot in search of a pay phone. He called the student group's mentor, who happened to be on his way south with his father, a Baptist minister, to see family in Mississippi. When they arrived at our house early the next morning, my mother was an emotional mess. She believed that this had been their only chance to extricate Ewan and that it had failed miserably. The mentor's father offered to pray with her and she agreed. My father, on the other hand, was angry at having to hand over his son to these two, and wished he could do something, perhaps something violent, to stop it.

We didn't see my brother again for nine months. He was emotionally devastated. He cut off all communication, giving only occasional updates through friends. To save enough money to pay for his last year of college himself, he took a year off and lived in the Zoo and didn't come home for Christmas. "For the first time, I did not feel safe at home," he said. "And that was part of what was emotionally devastating. But the lake house, as far as I was concerned, ended our relationship as it existed for the last twenty years. I could no longer trust them."

My parents were devastated, too, my mother's sadness exacerbated by the loss of a cherished pet and my impending exit for college. But less than a year later, things began to thaw. Dissatisfied with life in the Zoo, which had become more intentional and restrictive, Ewan left. No one resisted. He came to my high school graduation that spring, and in August he called and said he wanted to meet our parents and me in Washington so he could introduce us to his girlfriend, Kathy, who was also a member of the student group. Six weeks later they eloped, and they've been married ever since.

] [

My parents' relationship with Ewan remained strained for many years after that, and I honestly don't know if they ever made peace with his decision to become a Christian. Near the end of her life, desperate for some solace from terminal illness, Mama went to him for spiritual guidance. Near the end of his, when asked about his religious beliefs, Daddy told my sister-in-law that he considered it a matter best kept private. But hearing my brother describe those five years of family combat, I realized how little I had understood about what he had gone through. I had been captive to our parents' version of events and never bothered to ask his side of the story. I didn't believe he was any less to blame for the anger and bitterness that enveloped our family than they were. But his faith he had come by honestly. I could no more ask him to change his beliefs than he could ask me to alter mine. Simply by accepting that his worldview might have some legitimacy and wasn't a threat seemed to defuse two and a half decades of tension. Our differences weren't going to go away, but they didn't have to drive us further apart. Over lunch several days after our father's memorial service, he told me that I was his hero because I had taken Daddy in when he could no longer live alone. It dawned on me that perhaps he didn't think less of me simply because of my lack of faith. I owed him the same respect.

When he had finished retelling his saga, Ewan thanked me. "I don't think anyone's ever asked me to tell that whole story before," he said. I wished I hadn't waited so long.

[*six*]

LIFE GROUP

After three years living back in my hometown, Cristina and I decided our little family should move. We had many close friends in Charlotte but had never felt completely at ease there. The city seemed too crowded, too corporate, too homogeneous. Besides, I had left my job and was now freelancing full-time, so we could live anywhere we wanted. On a lark, we went to see a house that was for sale two and a half hours away in Chapel Hill, home to the University of North Carolina, where Cristina and I had met and fallen for each other. Like most college towns, it's a magnet for liberals, intellectuals, and bohemians. Jesse Helms had once suggested that instead of building a new state zoo, "we just fence in that one they have in Chapel Hill." One evening after we had settled into our new home, while Cristina was at her book club, I lay watching television in the blissfully vegetative state that follows getting two children bathed, in bed, and asleep without spousal assistance. When she returned, she walked into the den and sat down on the arm of the couch. My eyes not straying from the TV screen, I asked how it had gone.

—We're all nothing.

—Huh?

—We went around the room. We're all nothing.

She and her friends had been discussing their religious affiliations. Turns out none of them had one. Seven women in their thirties and forties, all curious, intelligent, and cultured, but not a single one identified with a community of faith, at least not yet.

We were home.

[ ]

My brother's conversion had put our parents on the defensive about their lack of a spiritual life of their own and the influence that might have had upon us. They questioned whether their disinterest in organized religion and disdain of excesses in its name had backfired and turned him in the completely opposite direction. They wondered whether they had been lazy or undisciplined or too permissive. They decided they needed to find a place where they could work out their feelings about his rebellion and maybe in the process show him that they weren't Godless Heathens after all. They decided to go back to church.

A high school sophomore at the time, I was expected, at least tacitly, to join them. It was no secret that we were motivated by family harmony and not any resurgence of faith. We were like a couple that goes shopping for a puppy in the hopes of saving a troubled relationship: The real goal is peace on the home front. You know sooner or later that dog's going to wind up back at the pound. But we did it anyway, donning dress clothes on Sunday mornings to sample the handful of liberal and middle-of-the-road mainline Protestant churches our city had to offer. I actually never minded. I found it vaguely thrilling to put on a suit and tie and head over to the more affluent side of town, where most of these churches were, and the whole production seemed to have a calming effect on all of us. It felt like we were finally doing what we were supposed to, what was socially acceptable. After some months of this, we settled on a bookish Presbyterian congregation that included several of my father's colleagues from the university. In many ways, it was the perfect choice. The church looked like a church was supposed to, its redbrick façade and white steeple stately and solid, its grounds well maintained but not manicured. The senior pastor was more storyteller than sermonizer, a revered man in his seventies with a love of literature and a sonorous southern baritone, and the theological discussions tended to be intellectual and comfortably abstract.

But if churchgoing took with my parents, at no point over the next several years did I witness any welling up of spirituality. As far as I could tell, nothing had changed, except that before we hadn't gone to church and now we did. The people of Trinity Presbyterian Church were warm and welcoming and caring from our first visit, and it did not take long for my parents to find comfort and make friends they would have for the rest of their lives. They sought counseling from the pastor and were reassured that they were not bad parents. I felt comfortable, too. Two girls from my school were members, and we sometimes sat together in the back so we could whisper or play hangman in the margins of our bulletin. I joined the youth group and, with my mother's encouragement, signed up for confirmation class and acolyte training. By my senior year, I was hoisting the shiny metal crucifix above my shoulders and walking it up the gray stone aisle at the beginning of the service (and back down again at the end). Before I was confirmed and made a member of the church, I was required to make a statement of faith in front of the session. I don't remember what I said, only that my mother described it to a friend as "fairly secular."

At services, my mind always wandered. The names and places in the Scripture readings were in a foreign language, and I was constantly losing track of the minister's point during the sermon. It was as if I had been inoculated already against the Christian message. Still, I sang the hymns, said the Lord's Prayer, and when the time came for a silent reflection, after the offering plates had circulated,

I ritually shut my eyes, lowered my chin to just below my neck, and offered up the same meek plea: *God, if You exist, let me know Your love and help me to show it to those around me.* Did I feel a connection to God, or to my fellow worshippers, heads also bowed in prayer? I can't recall feeling anything but comfort and belonging among all those friendly, well-meaning, like-minded people, the way one feels sitting in a crowded theater as the credits roll at the end of a particularly good movie. *Yes, that felt good. I'm glad we came. Much better than sloughing around the house in our pajamas and slippers all morning.* Slowly I'd open my eyes, raise my head, look at my mother, and we would both smile. I'd pat her hand a few times or squeeze it with mine and hope that she was as content as I was. A few more minutes of silence and then a jolt to the eardrums from the organ playing those first bright notes of the Doxology and the ushers marching down the aisle in their wingtips and pumps. As we remained standing, the pastor would say the charge and benediction, sending us back into the world stronger and more at peace. And then it was off to the parlor. *Following today's worship, please join us in the parlor for coffee and fellowship.* Oh, how I loved the parlor, so warm and cozy and garrulous, its carpeted floor and upholstered furniture the ultimate reward for sitting so long in the stark cold and quiet of the sanctuary. It was what kept me coming back to Trinity. The adoring, loving hugs from the middle-aged mothers; the proud, briefly paralyzing handshakes from fathers; the jokes and snickers with friends, liberated from the hushed seriousness of the pastor's deep-throated sermon, all of it giving reassurance that, yes, in fact, you belonged. Oh, how I loved the parlor.

][

The concept that our thoughts and actions have consequences is crucial to Christianity, with its promise of eternal life for true believers and eternal damnation for everyone else. If you don't think hell is real, then you probably don't spend a lot of time worrying about having to relocate there when you die. Besides, if you're wrong, all your favorite bands will be there, too.

But a lack of religion can have serious consequences in the here and now, if you believe a growing body of academic work. Lately researchers have churned out study after study attempting to determine if religious belief and activity can boost our physical and emotional well-being. And much to the chagrin of us Nones, most of the studies have found that the correlation of the two is positive. Take just one example: In a study of the longevity of 20,000 Americans, white men and women who reported that they went to church regularly lived an average of seven years longer than those who said they didn't. For African-Americans in the study, the average faith-based increase in life expectancy was fourteen years. In general, studies show that the less religious you are, the less healthy you are, and the more religious you are, the more healthy, says Dr. Harold Koenig, co-director of the Center for Spirituality, Theology and Health at Duke University Medical Center.

A leading figure in the study of religion and health, Koenig has authored or coauthored forty books and more than three hundred peer-reviewed articles and book chapters. He's also a member of a Charismatic church and the author of a book called *The Healing Power of Faith*. In September 2008, he testified before Congress that studies have linked religion and spirituality to lower rates of stroke, faster recovery from cardiac surgery, lower blood pressure, better immune/endocrine functioning, improved outcomes from HIV/AIDS, lower risk of and better outcomes from cancer, less susceptibility to infection, and slower progression of Alzheimer's disease and other cognitive disabilities due to aging. Drawing more specific conclusions about the health of an atheist versus that of a theist, an unchurched versus a churchgoing person, poses some difficulty, Koenig told me. Mainly because of the difficulty of identifying a sufficient number of subjects, there haven't been any studies focused on the health of nonbelievers.

But in a society obsessed with living longer, more fulfilling lives, this seems to me to be a critical question. How many of us spiritual fence-sitters would drag our butts to church every week if we knew it would add a few extra years to our lives or make the ones we have left a little better? Wouldn't Oprah be hounding us every day to make sure we give it up to God? Wouldn't doctors be oath-bound to prescribe double doses of Communion wafers? Then again, Jesus didn't die so that you could shave a few points off your bad cholesterol. Are these consequences truly reasons to think and act more religiously?

Right off the bat, one reason religion and health appear to go together is obvious: In many faiths, potentially risky behaviors such as drinking and smoking are discouraged if not downright forbidden. It's no coincidence that Seventh-Day Adventists and Mormons are among the longest-living groups of Americans. But even when the dimension of social control is factored out, religion and health appear to be highly correlated. Koenig told me that a National Institutes of Health review of the field in 2005, which was led by a religious skeptic, found that typically 25 percent of the difference in health remained after controlling for all relevant psychological, behavioral, and social variables. Of course, research of this kind typically doesn't show causality. It's impossible to determine, for instance, if a practicing Catholic is healthier than the lapsed one because of God or just good genes. Religious participation is generally a better predictor of good health than mere belief or spirituality. In fact, the more activity, the better. But one prominent scholar recently penned an article that declared church attendance a "black box" for health researchers.

But there is one element of religious participation that is widely thought to be beneficial to health, and that nonreligious people may be more likely to miss out on, which is social capital. Social capital is simply the act of engaging with other people and all of its attendant benefits that was famously described by Harvard political scientist Robert Putnam in the book *Bowling Alone*. In communities with high levels of social capital, according to Putnam, people connect frequently with others, forming valuable bonds based on "norms of reciprocity, mutual assistance and trustworthiness." Putnam's thesis was that Americans' involvement in the networks that generate social capital—civic associations, recreational groups, volunteer organizations—has fallen dramatically since the 1960s, which he took as a bad omen for our democracy.

I had studied Putnam's research in graduate school, and it resonated with me. And yet, like many time-starved, stressed-out people, I have a shocking social capital deficit. I'm not a member of any service clubs or sports leagues.

I'm not active in local politics or government. I don't really have many hobbies or interests over which I might bond with others. So I was interested in how this might affect my health. According to Koenig, with social capital also comes support and encouragement in the face of illness, reinforcement of a sense of meaning and purpose in life, exposure to information about healthy behaviors and opportunities for reinforcement, and more and stronger social ties and friendships, which have been shown to correlate highly with longevity. This is especially critical later in life, when researchers think it can provide support when parents, spouses, or coworkers are no longer able to. And churches are classic sources of social capital, knitting people together based on common values and aspirations and doing it through a variety of meaningful and enduring modes of engagement. Indeed, churches provide networks within networks: Sunday school classes, Bible studies, youth groups, singles groups, volunteer teams, small groups—they all generate social capital. By contrast, while there are atheist, humanist, and free-thought groups in every city in America, they tend to be small and fragmented. They can't foster connection and support to the same degree that churches do, which leaves Nones relatively isolated, especially late in life. I had seen this firsthand. For my parents, returning to church had provided a booster shot of social capital. They attended book discussions and weekend retreats. My mother volunteered for the church's Habitat for Humanity team and a group that supported people with HIV and AIDS. My father served as an elder. When my parents got sick, the bonds they formed in these activities were a critical source of support. Says Koenig: "Atheists probably do as well as everybody else does when they're young and healthy. The issues come up when you get sick and lose loved ones and lose your ability to control your life and you face suffering."

At the same time researchers have been broadening their inquiry into the links between religion and physical health, they've also begun investigating whether there might be a connection with psychological well-being, that is, happiness. Happiness is the holy grail for the modern American. We are obsessed with achieving self-actualization, work-life balance, and inner peace, and the purported sources of such contentment are increasingly the subject of study in the scientific community. If we can't be happy as we are, then perhaps research will tell us what it is we lack so that we can go about trying to acquire it. Not surprisingly, the impact of religion is one of the key targets of happiness research, and once again, the results have not been very good for those of us who don't have one. Koenig rattled off another list: People who attend church regularly report lower levels of stress, are at less risk of depression, make speedier recoveries from emotional disability, and report higher levels of quality of life and contentment.

The reasons behind this, researchers speculate, mirror the associations between religion and physical health. For instance, social activity of the kind that faith communities offer is thought to contribute significantly to a person's happiness, particularly later in life. Religion provides many with a sense of meaning or purpose in their lives, support in times of stress, and mechanisms for coping with difficulties in their lives such as prayer. One recent study suggested a link with self-control. Even my aunt's assertion that religion is a source of self-esteem may be empirically true: After interviewing eight hundred Americans over the age of sixty-five, sociologists Neil Krause and Christopher Ellison found that the more people were encouraged to be religious by their parents when they were children, the stronger their feelings of self-worth now, as much as sixty years later.

Of course, the problem is not just that, as a result of missing out on all of the salutary effects of faith, nonreligious Americans like me are less content than we could be. Our happiness quotient is also depressed by alienation. Despite the growth of the Nones over the last two decades, living without religion is still perceived by many as an unacceptable, perhaps un-*American*, way of life. In

2003, a group of researchers from the University of Minnesota included several questions about atheists in a larger study of diversity in society called the American Mosaic Project. The results were published in an article in the *American Sociological Review*, the title of which gives you a pretty good idea of what they found: "Atheist as 'Other': Moral Boundaries and Cultural Membership in American Society." Nearly 40 percent of the people they polled said that atheists didn't share their "vision of American society," and nearly half said they would disapprove if their child wanted to marry an atheist. On these two topics, atheists fared the worst of the minority groups the survey asked about. Only 26.3 percent and 33.5 percent of respondents, respectively, answered the same for Muslims. "It is striking that the rejection of atheists is so much more common than rejection of other stigmatized groups," the researchers wrote. "Americans construct the atheist as the symbolic representation of one who rejects the basis for moral solidarity and cultural membership in American society altogether."

Of course, that's just how Will Herberg described Americans' view of Nones back in the mid-1950s. He believed we were "not even remotely significant in determining the American's understanding of himself," he wrote. "Not to be a Catholic, a Protestant, or a Jew today is, for increasing numbers of American people, not to be anything, not to have a *name*." The difference in the intervening years is how drastically perceptions of other "others," including religious minorities, have changed. Over the last forty years, even as America has become more diverse, it has become more comfortable with its diversity. And faith groups have become more comfortable with—indeed some have become champions of—religious pluralism. Building on Herberg's "common faith" and "belief in belief," differences among religions have been de-emphasized in pursuit of common social or political goals. But this growing acceptance has yet to be extended to nonbelievers. At the outset of the 2008 presidential campaign, the Gallup Poll tried to gauge Americans' willingness to accept candidates of different race, religious background, age, and marital status. To the question "If your party nominated a generally well-qualified person who happened to be atheist, would you vote for that person," only 45 percent said yes, while 53 percent said no. Since the last time the question was asked, in 1999, the proportion of Americans who would accept an atheist candidate had actually declined, from 49 percent, and, once again, the hypothetical nonbeliever trailed all others in the survey, including "a woman," "a Mormon," "72 years of age," "married for the third time," and "a homosexual."

But numbers like those tell only part of the story. Americans have a long history of demonizing nonbelievers.

Atheism was linked with communism during the days of the Red Scare, and in the 1980s, the Moral Majority declared secular humanists "Public Enemy Number One" and blamed them for the demise of prayer and the teaching of sex education in public schools. "They claimed we were part of a conspiracy that controlled the liberal foundations, the universities, the media," I was told by Paul Kurtz, who founded the organization now known as the Council for Secular Humanism in response to the attacks. Even today, six states, including North Carolina, still have laws on the books keeping nonbelievers from holding public office, and divorced parents have lost custody cases for failing to provide "spiritual education" for their children. All of that is bound to have an impact on a person's self-worth. When Canadian psychologists Bruce E. Hunsberger and Bob Altemeyer surveyed three hundred members of atheist organizations in San Francisco, Idaho, and Alabama, the largest such study ever done, they asked subjects to describe how they came to nonbelief. For many, it was an opportunity to document the ugly reactions their atheism has produced, including hatred, discrimination, and abuse, and the lengths to which they have gone to keep their nonbelief to themselves. In the 2006 book that detailed their research, *Atheism: A Groundbreaking Study of America's Nonbelievers,* Hunsberger and Altemeyer summarized forty of these sad stories:

"People assume you're heartless, shallow, amoral, and it calls their own beliefs into question. Atheism *greatly* disturbs people."

"In the United States, the default position is 'believer.' I learned to never assert atheism. It's sort of like burning the flag."

"When I wear a t-shirt with an atheist slogan, I get a verbal attack."

"I've had to remove an atheist sticker from the rear of my scooter because car drivers would try to run me off the road, screaming 'Jesus is Lord.' And police would pull me over and check my papers for no reason."

"My non-religious 'coming-out' was far worse than a gay friend's coming out to his parents. It took eight years to get a better relationship with my parents."

"To this day my in-laws consider me the 'anti-Christ' and refuse to talk to me."

"I have had crosses planted in my yard, my kids have been harassed at school, I've been a victim of religious discrimination at work, my car has been vandalized, I've received death threats via e-mail, mail and under my windshield wipers."

As with any claim to victimization, it's possible to over-play anecdotes like these. They certainly don't constitute evidence of widespread or systemic persecution of athe-ists. And as the number of nonreligious people in America grows, their feelings of alienation may lessen. The recent popularity of books by atheists suggests the stigma is al-ready losing its power.

But you have to wonder how far we've come since 1964, when *Life* magazine called American Atheists leader Madalyn Murray O'Hair "the most hated woman in Amer-ica." O'Hair delighted in that honor, just as she took glee in the controversy that her crusades against religion gener-ated. She made enemies among nonbelievers, too, and battles over power and money would ultimately destroy the organization she started. I had never heard of O'Hair until I was working as a newspaper reporter in Austin, where she had lived until disappearing with her son and granddaughter in 1995. She wasn't found for six years, when the man who kidnapped and killed her and her fam-ily led police to their remains, which were buried on a South Texas ranch, and when the news broke, my col-leagues and I crowded around the TV set in the newsroom to hear the gory details. Madalyn Murray O'Hair wasn't murdered because she was an atheist. But the circumstances of her life and death make me doubt she was a very *happy* person.

] [

Perhaps the best example of how religion can foster social capital can be seen at Saddleback Church, the Southern California mega-church led by Rick Warren, author of the Purpose-Driven Life series of bestsellers. In a 2005 article in *The New Yorker,* Malcolm Gladwell described how Saddleback has used groups of eight or ten to connect its tens of thousands of members. In a mega-church, where members might never meet the pastor or know more than a small portion of the congregation, small groups are the only way to get the regular, face-to-face contact that will encourage and support them in their faith. In other words, they're a major source of social capital (and one that Robert Putnam and coauthor Lewis Feldstein profiled in a later book on exemplars of the concept, *Better Together*). In a given week, 30,000 people attend Saddleback small groups, which is more than attend the weekend services. For Saddleback, and most all Evangelical churches large and small, there was no better way of building active communities of believers whose lives are connected at a deep level. "Today, at least forty million Americans are in a religiously based small group, and the growing ranks of small-group membership have caused a profound shift in the nature of the American religious experience," Gladwell wrote.

I had heard my brother mention his family's membership over the years in different small groups, or "care groups," as they're sometimes called, but I was clueless as to what went on in them. After reading about Saddleback, I wanted to see firsthand the inner workings of what went on in these little engines of social capital. So I contacted the pastor of the largest Evangelical church in Chapel Hill, which is known to locals as simply "the Bible Church." Theologically conservative and nondenominational, it held its first gatherings in buildings on campus but now attracts about fifteen hundred people each Sunday to a gleaming eight-year-old facility on the way to Durham and Duke University. In the über-liberal confines of a college town, a suburban-style mega-church is downright countercultural. A neighbor of mine once referred to it as "that country club for Christians." But the Bible Church is actually a model of diversity, counting liberals and conservatives, blacks and whites, and forty different nationalities among its members. I told the pastor that while I wasn't thinking about joining, I was interested in learning more about how Christians lived out their faiths. I suggested one way I could do this was to sit in on one of his church's small groups. To my surprise, he thought it was a great idea, just the kind of engagement with non-Christians he was always encouraging his church to do more of. The following week, I got a brief e-mail from Brian, a young business development executive who had been a member of the Bible Church for about eight years. He and his wife, Wesley, led a small group for young couples that met every other Tuesday at their house, "to connect, reflect on scripture together, and generally just share life," his e-mail said, and I was welcome to join them anytime. The Bible Church calls its small groups "Life Groups," and there are more than fifty from which to choose, including Life Groups for men, women, young adults, parents of preschoolers, fathers and sons, parents of twentysomethings, people who are into drama, people who want to play tennis, speakers of Chinese, and speakers of Korean. For a church its size, that's not a very big number: Saddleback has more than thirty-six hundred small groups. The group I had latched on to officially had five other couples. They included two medical school graduates doing their residencies, an MBA student, a physical therapist, a nurse, and a firefighter. They met on Tuesday evenings, and before my first visit, Brian and I met for a beer at a sports bar. Afterward I got another e-mail from him. "Thanks for being courageous to hang out with mostly strangers and living honestly with us," he wrote. "Don't be bashful: add your comments, ask hard questions, and have fun."

Devout Christians are stereotyped as pushy, self-righteous, judgmental, and dull, the last person an unchurched person like me would want to spend time with. But within minutes of us meeting, Brian had shown himself to be quite the opposite. He was agreeable, open-minded, interesting, and engaging. Our backgrounds and our outlooks were completely different, but I could imagine us being friends. I had mentioned to one of my brother's friends, a Christian, that I was joining this group, and he had jokingly asked if I was worried about being the target of proselytizing. When I told Brian that, he said I had nothing to worry about. Converting me wasn't his job, it was God's. All he could do was show me an example of someone trying to live out the tenets of Christian faith and hope that I saw some value in doing the same. *Of course, that's exactly what you would say if you were trying to convert someone and didn't want him to suspect anything.*

I was the last one to arrive at their Cape Cod in a quiet wooded subdivision in Durham. The others were standing around the crowded kitchen, waiting for Brian to return from his six-year-old daughter's soccer practice. It was his birthday, and his four-year-old son sat at the table eating cake Wesley had made. He showed up a few minutes after me, a wiry thirty-five-year-old with a broad smile and self-deprecating manner, and we all lingered for a while in the kitchen. They joked about sports and politics, asked about job searches or pregnancies or exercise regimens, and generally caught up on one another's lives since the last time they had gathered. They had been meeting for eighteen months at that point and were comfortable enough with one another to laugh about sketches from *Saturday Night Live* that they watched online or when Wesley told them that the cake she had made was called "Better Than Sex." I began to wonder how much I was going to learn from people who seemed so normal.

After singing "Happy Birthday," we relocated to couches and chairs in the large living room. Brian, who would lead the group's Bible study that evening, sat on the floor against the fireplace hearth and stretched his legs in front of him. They had been slogging through Galatians for more than a year, and they were coming to the end. But before that could begin, one couple made an announcement that quickly cast a pall over everyone else. They were feeling the strain of having a new baby and the husband's long hours at work and had decided that they needed to take a break from the group until their schedules eased up. But they weren't even planning to stay that night, having already told their babysitter they would be home shortly. The others, while sympathetic, clearly didn't want to lose two core members of their group when they were already struggling to maintain a critical mass. Wesley led everyone in a short prayer for the couple before they left; later, she and

Brian would talk with them by phone and encourage them to stick with the group, even if it meant moving it to a different night. "The thing I expressed to them later was that we're all tempted to 'unplug' when life gets overwhelming, but that what we've been studying in Galatians should give them the freedom to live messy with us, not put on a show, and have folks who will walk with them through the tough stuff," Brian told me in an e-mail. "I've always found that once you 'unplug' it's much harder to get the gumption to plug back in again and be known by folks."

When conversation turned back to the Bible study, the enthusiasm and conviviality with which they had mingled in the kitchen had drained out of the room. Brian set up the passage, reminding everyone about the context and the verses leading up to it, and then asked Wesley to read it aloud. Often described as "the Magna Carta of Christian freedom," Galatians is Paul's powerful rebuke of the Christians in a region of what is now Turkey, who had succumbed to the belief that in order to follow Christ, they must follow the religious customs of the Jews, such as circumcision. Paul derided the notion that Christians need do anything but show faith in God, and that the legalism of the Galatian church, just as of the Pharisees in Jesus' time, would only divide God's children and sacrifice the unity and freedom that Jesus died for. When Wesley was finished, Brian turned to the seven questions in the study guide. Maybe it was the concern for the couple leaving the group, maybe it was the study guide's didactic tone— "According to this passage, what are the two natures at work in every Christian?" was the first question—but I felt Brian struggling mightily to stimulate discussion. I was immediately aware of the difference in age and life stage that separated him and Wesley from the rest of the group. I couldn't tell if the others were straining to apply this serious-minded lesson to their own lives, or were they just not particularly interested in this part of Life Group activities. Brian asked if anyone had an example of wanting something so badly that the desire overtakes you and you lose sight of the reason you wanted it in the first place. He offered his own, a recent obsession with replacing their home computer, which had led to his drooling over the possibilities at the store and forgetting the real need, not to mention all of the other, more important things he could spend his family's time and money on. That's what happened to the Galatians when they had become obsessed with legalism. It was a nice, accessible analogy, but it got almost no traction with the group. I hesitated to answer, too, not wanting to look like the teacher's pet. My only comment was to note that in my Revised Standard Version, this passage contained the word "fornication." Awkward silence followed and I decided to shut up.

The Bible study felt like a tutoring session for busy

young Christians. Brian lobbed questions and little in the way of answers came back. There was no dissent or debate, no thought-provoking back-and-forth, in short, none of the spiritual and intellectual nourishment I expected to see dished out in the small group setting. I'm not saying they weren't sincerely attempting to study the Bible and understand the meaning of a vital section of it, or that they weren't trying to engage with one another. But toward the end of the evening, when Wesley asked for prayer requests, the tone shifted back. Once more, the conversation began to flow, as each member of the group had a chance to unload his or her most pressing concerns, with the knowledge that the rest of the group would be psychically helping bear those burdens over the next two weeks. They asked one another to pray that a sinus infection would clear up, that a job interview would go smoothly, that tension at work would ease, and that couples would find time in their hectic schedules to connect. No problem seemed too small, yet viewed in context, none of their worries were trivial in the slightest. They were the authentic struggles that these people were facing. They just weren't the venues in which I would expect to find God intervening. Of course, not believing in God, I'm an outlier in this group.

What I had seen that night had surprised me, but it actually seemed to support the social capital notion. Galatians was practically a diversion, despite Brian's best efforts to tie it together with what was happening in their busy lives. Clearly, what was holding this group together, however tenuously, was community. In a congregation as large as the Bible Church, these people might otherwise not know one another, might not even see one another in church even if they did. The Life Group didn't just harness the power of familiarity, it actually generated more of it every time they came together.

I vowed to arrive at the second meeting better prepared. I didn't want to just go through the motions; I wanted to try being an active participant. So instead of just reading the passage and printing out the questions, I wrote out my answers. The passage centered on the notion of conceit and how it naturally leads people to be either jealous or scornful of one another, instead of having the humility and boldness to lift each other up. As Paul chides, "For if any one thinks he is something, when he is nothing, he deceives himself." When we got to question seven, which asks why Christians do so poorly at being humble and bearing one another's burdens, I changed "Christians" to "the unchurched" and had no trouble filling out a nice long list. When it was time for prayer requests, Wesley reminded us she was having difficulty keeping up with homeschooling in addition to the responsibilities of mother and homemaker. Earlier, after describing this struggle for a few minutes, she stopped, perhaps worrying that she was being self-indulgent with her gripes, and made fun of herself in a way that I found totally endearing: "The point is, I'm self-absorbed and I need Jesus!" Yet it was clear that what she probably needed just as much was this kind of social capital–generating activity to support and encourage her. Heck, we all could. When it was my turn, I decided that it was only polite to participate. So I offered up a bit sheepishly that Cristina was going back to work for the first time since having children, and that I was struggling to make headway on my book, and that we could probably use help on both fronts. I had never asked anyone to pray for me before. But I figured it couldn't hurt, even if, or maybe especially if, we weren't doing it ourselves, and I have to admit, it felt nice. I came home and told Cristina not to worry about her new job. She was being prayed for.

I made it only one more time after that. My own schedule was starting to get in the way, and a comment from the last get-together had stuck in my craw. Discussing some of the issues she was struggling with, one member mentioned that she had "hung out with a bunch of non-Christians and that didn't lift me up." *Well, excuse me*. Besides, we were finished with the Galatians study and the holidays were approaching. After we wrapped up, I lingered in the living room talking with Brian and we watched a few minutes of the presidential debate on the television. He invited me to stay and watch the whole thing, but I wondered if it might be uncomfortable, since we seemed to be as far apart politically as we were spiritually. I said my good-byes, mentioning on the way out that we should get together for a beer or to play tennis sometime. A few months later, I called Brian at home to catch up: We hadn't spoken since my last time with the Life Group, and to my surprise, it had disbanded shortly thereafter. They had moved the meeting to Sunday nights in hopes of keeping the stressed-out couple who had decided to leave. But then other couples started to have trouble making it. The MBA student accepted a job offer with a consulting firm in Chicago. The physical therapist had her baby. The firefighter and nurse bought a house in the country that needed work. Brian took it in stride. He knew from past experience that there's a "life cycle" to small groups and that, periodically, people need an opportunity to bow out. The circumstances that were making it difficult to get this group together signaled to him that he needed to provide just such an opportunity. That was okay, though: He and Wesley were planning to convene a new one in the fall.

[*seven*]

THANK YOU

It's taken for granted in America that having a child is a life change that drives people to church. There are militant atheists who after becoming parents never again miss a Sunday service. They treat religion as if it's just one more novel facet of parenthood—like knowing what a doula is or joining the La Leche League—or a requirement of their newfound role as upstanding members of society. Perhaps it's just the realization that they're suddenly expected to lead another human being from the larval stage of life all the way to college graduation that sends them running in search of a higher power. Some parents try to inculcate faith in their kids even when they themselves have none. After directing a documentary about Evangelicals, filmmaker Alexandra Pelosi decided that the son she was expecting would be taken to church, despite her own misgivings about organized religion. "Because if I don't," she told a reporter, "he will be called 'unchurched' and [those are the people] most susceptible to some of the more extreme religions later in life. You have to give your children something that they can reject if they want to."

After analyzing survey data collected in two time periods—1972 to 1976, and 1998 to 2002—Princeton University sociologist Robert Wuthnow concluded that there's almost no better way of determining how frequently people go to church than by counting the number of booster seats in the back of their car. In both eras, married people with one child went more than those with no children, and those with two more than those with just one. Even more telling, among parents with three or more children, men were just as likely to go to church as women, closing the persistent gender gap in church attendance. If Will Herberg was right in his crediting postwar American religiosity to middle-class desires for social acceptability, this pattern is surely evidence for it. Or perhaps starting a family simply changes one's perspective on religion and what it can provide for those who have a healthy dose of it. Plenty of research lately has shown that kids of religious parents are less likely to turn into risk-taking antisocial teenagers. "Having children and wanting to set a good example for them is one of the reasons adults go to church," Wuthnow writes. "As one young woman remarked, 'I'm not that sure about church for myself, but I want my children to have that exposure.'" I knew people who fell into the same category as that woman, particularly men who had once displayed no faith at all but now attended church regularly at their wives' behest. I would have done the same had Cristina asked, but she never did. We worried that traditional Christianity was too intertwined with traditional parenting in a way that made us uncomfortable. "He who spares the rod hates his son," says Proverbs 13:24. And just as with corporal punishment, we found it hard to budge on the issue of churchgoing on the basis of convention, even when other parents looked at us as if we were crazy for agonizing over this choice. *It's an hour a week,* I could imagine them saying.

Still, I tended to see religion through the prism of family life, too—as a social outlet, support network, educational opportunity, and more. But what about for those of us who decide that organized religion isn't for us? Organizations for atheists and humanists have been around for decades, many with local chapters that have regular meetings. But they've always been short on the kind of activities that matter to families. It's simple demographics: Historically, the nonreligious have been disproportionately male and single, which means in general they're not likely to care much about playdates and pizza parties. I found myself wishing we could still access the benefits of belonging to a church: the rituals and celebrations, the teaching of values and ethics, the community, the fun T-shirts. Churches serve it all up like potato salad at a picnic.

Parenting is an inherently neurotic affair, and I'm convinced that we have far less control over the outcome of our children's lives than we think we do. None of us knows how they are going to turn out and if we will ultimately regret one parenting technique or another. And yet even if we accept that, it's not like we're going to throw up our hands and do nothing, vainly hoping none of our offspring winds up in prison. At the Vacation Bible School that my friend May sends her children to for a week in the summer, the kids spend one day on each of several key values, such as trust, respect, and honesty. When I heard this, I neurotically wondered what Cristina and I were doing to instill those principles in our children. Would they wind up less trustworthy as a result?

] [

One fall weekend when our son was still a baby, we took him with us to meet some friends in the mountains of North Carolina. He probably wasn't quite old enough to make such a journey, which required flying from Dallas to Charlotte and then a few hours' drive in a friend's car. Barely three months old, he demanded, it seemed, almost constant nursing. On the last stretch of highway, hoping to avoid yet another pit stop, Cristina resorted to dangling her engorged breast over his mouth so he could suckle as he lay strapped into his car seat, passing motorists be damned. This was the second time that year we had gathered with this group of high school classmates of mine and significant others. The first one took place on a weekend that "straddled" January and February, so we began referring to it as "the Straddle Retreat," or just "Straddle," and vowed to make it an annual affair. It seemed like a good metaphor for our station in life—one foot still in childhood, the other stepping gingerly into grown-up-ville. For a few days each year, we would forgo the small talk that typically consumed such reunions and instead try to connect on a deeper level. The agenda included hikes in the woods, family-style meals, and long, ponderous discussions about the meaning of life. Really. The thing about Straddle is that it's impossible to describe it without sounding horribly pretentious, which, I guess, we were. But it was a weekend that we anticipated with excitement every time it came around.

This time, bleary from all the sleepless nights, I would have been happy just to have an adult conversation or two. But a few days before we left, Cristina suggested that our friend David, who had followed his father into the ministry and was working as a chaplain at a small college, could perform a blessing of some sort for our son. She had posed this idea in the form of a question—"What would you think if we . . ."—but I knew from the deliberate way she asked it that she had already arrived at the answer. I paused long enough to do a quick brain scan for arguments against. I had nothing. In fact, months before, when we had discussed whether or not to baptize our still in utero child, I had been the one in favor of it. As was my wont in discussions such as these, I came down on the side of doing what was conventional. It was only right that our baby be welcomed into the world with an event where neckties would be worn and photographs taken. I would accept nothing less for my firstborn. Besides, I pointed out helpfully, there might be gifts, maybe even cash. Then there was Cristina's side: With no religious affiliation, church community, or firm beliefs of our own, a baptism would be empty and meaningless. And we were lucky: Unlike some of our friends, our parents weren't nagging us to do it, as if "eternal salvation" were something to check off of our list of things to do when we got home from the hospital. My mother-in-law had never even mentioned baptism to us. Granted, as a good Catholic, she had the power to take matters into her own hands the first time she got the boy alone in the bathtub. And honestly, if that made her happy, so be it. But in a church, in front of God and everyone? It just didn't seem right, Cristina argued, and, as usual, I had agreed. So why now the sudden interest in offering our child up to the gods? Had her Catholic guilt come back when her milk came in? Was she worried that our son might wind up in limbo, as the Vatican had once taught happened to babies who perished before they were baptized? Was she reconsidering our laissez-faire approach to religion?

I didn't actually ask those questions out loud. Instead, I inquired gently about her motivations. "I just feel like we need to say thank you," she said. Thank you to whom? I asked. She didn't know. Maybe the universe. Maybe Buddha. Maybe God. All she knew was that we had been the recipient of a gift that was as close to perfect as any we would ever see and it might be good to express a bit of gratitude for that, out loud, in front of witnesses, the sooner, the better. What better place to do that than among people we loved, gathered together out of respect and admiration, with the help of a real-life man of the cloth in our midst who was all too happy to spend a weekend with the unchurched, perhaps the unbelieving, stay up way too late drinking from bottomless glasses of wine, and listen to us complain, often without dissenting, about the silliness that we found in religion.

Yet I was still hesitant about this idea. Minister or no minister, it seemed a bit do-it-yourself. I had no interest in marring my son's heretofore perfect infancy with anything less than what was right and proper and by the book. Trouble was, I had made precisely the same everybody-else-is-doing-it argument when the question of circumcision was before us and, despite coming out victorious that time, I wasn't sure I could win with it again. So after breakfast, as David and I sat in rocking chairs on the deck that hung out over a thick autumn canopy, I asked if he would consider blessing my child. Whatever that meant.

] [

The growth in the ranks of the nonreligious to include more women and young families has sparked interest in re-creating some of what organized religion offers—hold the prayers and Bible stories. There are Sunday schools where children are taught ethics and critical thinking. There are secular parenting networks that gather for pot-luck suppers and trips to the museum, and summer camps where kids of atheist parents can make lanyards without fear of being preached to. There are naming ceremonies during which nonreligious parents welcome their child into the world, as Cristina wanted to do for our son, and gatherings to celebrate holidays such as the Winter Solstice and Charles Darwin's birthday. Add it all up and it's a sliver of what churches offer. But it's a start, the beginnings of what one day could be a nationwide apparatus to support people who want to bring their children up outside the bounds of organized religion, something my parents certainly never had.

It seemed fitting that my first exposure to this nascent

movement would take place on the campus of Harvard University. Here lies the beating heart of godlessness in America. Harvard is one of only a handful of universities in the country to employ a chaplain of humanism, the philosophy that people can lead ethical, fulfilling lives and contribute to the greater good without believing in anything supernatural. The chaplaincy has existed for more than thirty years, but in the 1990s, a wealthy ninety-two-year-old alumnus read about it in a Harvard publication, decided he, too, was a humanist, and gave $800,000 to endow it as a permanent position. Each year, the humanist chaplaincy names a "Humanist of the Year," and this year, the recipient was Dale McGowan, an author whose book, *Parenting Beyond Belief: On Raising Ethical, Caring Kids Without Religion,* had become something of a hit among Heathens.

McGowan, forty-six, is an expert in neither child development nor religion. For most of his professional life, he was a music professor at a small Catholic college in the Midwest. One day, though, a group of students approached him for help starting a campus group for nonbelievers. He agreed, thinking it would be a good test of the college's commitment to free speech and critical thinking. They quickly attracted twenty-six members and invited the president of the Freedom From Religion Foundation to speak. Forty-five minutes before the talk was to begin, a security

guard locked them out. The students staged the first campus protest in the school's history, but the college was unmoved, and McGowan was caught in the middle. He
found his employer's hypocrisy repugnant, but he needed
a job to support his family. He decided he would keep
quiet but leave teaching the following year to try to make
a living as a writer, eventually moving to the suburbs of
Atlanta. Reading up on his background before I left for
the seminar, I found McGowan instantly compelling. Here
was a guy who believed above all that people should be
free to think as they pleased, and he wanted his students
to see that such a belief was viable anywhere in America.
He had been wrong, and worse, when his commitment to
this principle had been tested, he had flinched. He
wouldn't sacrifice his family's comfort and security for the
Culture Wars. He was, in other words, a regular guy. In
Atlanta, which is not known as a bastion of irreligion. I had
a feeling I was going to like him.

By the time I found Fong Auditorium, I was forty-five
minutes late for McGowan's talk, which would be followed
by a half-day seminar for parents. This wasn't quite the
setting I had expected for the august-sounding "16th Annual Alexander Lincoln Lecture," previously delivered by
Pulitzer Prize–winning biologist E. O. Wilson and U.S.
Representative Pete Stark, the only admitted atheist in
Congress. This felt more like where you'd hold an early-

morning section of Psych 101 if you were being realistic about college students' attendance habits. The steeply raked seating gave the place a cramped feeling, and the only door was at the very front. I put my head down, climbed the stairs, and found a seat in one of the back rows. Standing at the lectern, McGowan looked much like the picture I had seen on his website—salt-and-pepper hair, a goatee, gap-toothed grin. In a dark suit with an open-collared shirt, he had the relaxed posture of someone who had spent a career in front of a classroom.

I arrived just as he was describing what he calls "the central concern" of nonreligious parents: indoctrination. According to McGowan, we live in fear that we will end up inculcating in our children our own worldview, the very thing that we chastise religious parents for doing, and this fear paralyzes us. "I've had many nonreligious parents tell me that they are so fearful of indoctrinating their kids," he said, slightly incredulous, "that they haven't even told them what they believe." Well, that sounds familiar, I thought. Was that the reason my parents had always kept their religious beliefs under wraps? Was that what I was doing with my own children? Could the answer be as easy as not being afraid to tell them what to think?

Ah, the seminar has already begun! Tell me, Professor McGowan, this indoctrination you speak of, how is it done? How do I make sure my children grow up to be good, commit-

ted secular humanists at absolutely no risk of backsliding into
believing in a higher power? Just give me a moment to get out
my notebook so I can get all the steps down in the right order.
Okay, now go ahead . . .

"All parents can and should influence their children,
and that influence is bound to be huge," he said. "Influence becomes indoctrination only when you forbid them
to question what they receive from you. For extra insurance, you should explicitly invite them to do so."

Oh. So there's a difference between indoctrination and
influence. Indoctrination is in fact something to be avoided,
but influence is inevitable? McGowan explained that parents could no less keep from having an impact on what
their kids think than on the color of their eyes and the
language they speak. So we should strive to have a positive
influence while also teaching them to think and question
so that, eventually, they can make up their own minds
about what they believe. His children will be tempted to
imitate his view of religion, just like they have imitated his
political preferences, and that's fine, but they are also
learning how to look critically at their parents' views, ask
questions, and understand the reasons so that they can
form their own opinions. And then when they are tempted
to think or do the opposite of what he and his wife think,
they will make sure there are equally sound reasons behind it. "The one thing I value most in my own worldview

is that I came to it by myself. Why should I deprive my kids of that authenticity?"

I stopped listening for a moment. I was pretty sure that McGowan had just described exactly what I wanted for my own kids. But I had been so focused on filling this one hole in my parenting résumé that I had forgotten what my job was. I was responsible for helping them learn how to make it on their own. Religion might inform that education, or even inspire it, but it couldn't take the place of it. I had to believe that learning how to live honestly and authentically would give them all the comfort, security, and self-esteem they would ever need. Yes, I had always hated the idea of "letting them make up their own minds." It seemed like the ultimate parental cop-out, a euphemism for avoiding tough decisions and hard lessons while the kids got away with pretty much whatever they wanted to. It was the child-rearing philosophy that inevitably led to vagrancy and poor hygiene, and it was the reason why at one time I had been determined never to live in a college town. Kids raised in college towns invariably had as many piercings as they had IQ points. I had always expected my kids would grow up in an environment of greater conformity and social acceptability than I had, not less. And yet here we were in Chapel Hill. I had brought my family to a place where intellectual stimulation and free inquiry were valued above all else, and I was glad I had. Wasn't I going to have to accept the consequences of teaching them to think for themselves?

Long before we had children, I was playing poker with a group of guys, and one of them invited the rest of us to join him in smoking a joint on the back patio. "No, thanks," another said. "I stopped that when I had kids." He couldn't stomach being a bad example to his offspring. "Really?" one of the pot smokers retorted on his way outside. "I started smoking *more.*" I understood the impulse to correct defects in one's life when bringing a new one into the world. But I also understood, probably felt it in my heart, that remaining true to myself was the only way to survive the chaos that commences with parenthood. It was also the example I wanted to set. Would I ultimately view religion the same way, that to be a role model was to acknowledge your doubts and questions even if it meant your kids grew up without the certainty of their churchgoing peers? Or would I decide it was easier to just come up with a story to tell them? I still didn't know, but McGowan was giving me a bit more confidence in being myself.

] [

After he had finished his lecture and accepted his Lucite "Humanist of the Year" trophy, we took a break while a lunch of soft tacos and tortilla chips was set out on a table at the front of the room. I looked around. The crowd wasn't as big as I had expected, and it wasn't hard to pick out the parents in the audience from those whose interest was more academic. Snap judgments had always come easily to me, and I quickly sized up these earnest young moms and dads. Most had that slightly disheveled, forever casual look about them that says, "I used to be a nonconformist, but now that I've got kids, the best you're going to get from me is an ironic T-shirt and a pair of jeans." They hadn't been the homecoming king and queen in high school, they hadn't rushed fraternities or sororities in college, and they sure as hell weren't the shiny, happy suburban Stepford parents you saw pushing their overpriced strollers through the shopping mall. Then again, they weren't scary Goth-mothers and -fathers with their kids' names and faces tat-tooed up their forearms, either.

When Cristina and I first met, I was immediately taken by the quiet way she indulged her quirkiness and whimsy, the way she let her freak flag fly just a bit higher than those of most people I knew. I remember looking across at her in one of our grad school lectures and seeing her taking notes with a pen that was bright orange and shaped like a carrot. At times I had gravitated away from such benign misfittery, preferring instead the company of more conven-tional people, but the older I got, the more I found it en-dearing, like it was one of the things that made life worth living. The people at this seminar seemed like they'd be worth getting to know.

I stood up and introduced myself to a few of them. Sitting behind me was a mother who had just moved from Austin, where she had started a network of nonreligious parents who met for trips to the park and potluck dinners. Austin is known as an oasis of liberalism in the Lone Star State, but she and her husband had been put off by occasional proselytizing by Christians at his company. She was happy they had moved to the Boston area, which seemed friendlier to her kind. Nearby was a young couple who also were recent transplants. In Canada, they had been members of a conservative church but, having lost their faith, they were anxious to find a community of humanists in their new home. Another couple told me about the nonreligious naming ceremony they had held for their newborn baby, officiated by Harvard's humanist chaplain. Their religious parents had happily joined in. Running out of people to talk to, I loitered in the lobby. A mother of three sold educational toys that celebrated Darwinism under the name "Charlie's Playhouse" (one T-shirt read "Product of Natural Selection" and another "98% Chimpanzee"). On a counter were brochures advertising Camp Quest, a summer camp for children of freethinkers, and the Secular Student Alliance, a college group devoted to advancing the interests of the nonreligious. This was the kinder, gentler, kid-friendlier side of unbelief, less likely to make fun of someone else's faith or push a political agenda.

When we reconvened, McGowan began with a word of encouragement: "Relax," he said. "Things are actually going in our direction." Parenting is especially neurotic for those of us going against the grain of a religious society. It's easy for us to feel embarrassed or ashamed about the choice to keep our children out of church. But our timidity is totally unwarranted, he said. There are an estimated 9 million of us in the United States, and that number will only grow as the ranks of the secular keep growing. He quoted familiar numbers—the doubling of the percentage of the population with no affiliation, for instance—but his message was different from what I had heard elsewhere. Instead of a call to arms, it was an appeal to reason. Millions of American families weren't religious at all. Most of us are hiding in plain sight, indistinguishable from our more pious neighbors. We should feel more confident that we're doing right by our kids and society, no matter what convention or the Religious Right or some self-righteous relative might say. "Getting rid of fear and instilling confidence are a big part of what we do," he said of his books and seminars. His second point also got my attention: He said there was good that was lost when you threw out religion, and while that's necessary, he was jealous of some of the things that communities of faith could offer. I hadn't heard that from many in the anti-religion crowd.

His advice was not exactly radical. But if it was common sense, it was the kind of common sense that goes out the window when a group of people in the minority feel besieged. For instance, McGowan advocates exposing children to religion early and often, something many nonreligious parents are reluctant to do. Children who never get exposed to faith, whether by going to church with friends or relatives whom the parents trust, or learning about it in a book or a movie, or simply discussing it at the dinner table, well, those kids are being stunted, too, passively indoctrinated to think of religion as something off-limits and mysterious. "If you get the kids to age eighteen and they haven't seen the inside of a church, that's a problem," he said. We should take every opportunity to discuss religious concepts with our kids, he said, so that they'll understand them, be able to discuss them, and have a basis for making up their own minds about them. He had touched on this strategy in his talk earlier that day: "I let religious ideas and stories and claims wash over my kids from every direction—*every* direction, not a single one—and that's crucial. They hear about baby Jesus and baby Hercules in the same breath. Jehovah gets no more airtime or credence than the Everlasting Brahmin, and Jesus no more than

Mithras. Variety is the key. Then stand back and let them experiment with one worldview after another while building their thinking skills and their love of the truth."

Hearing this made me wonder if I was telling my children enough, encouraging them to question. I was pretty sure they were clueless about what it meant to pray, for example. Given the chance to make a wish, my daughter would put her hands together, look up to the sky, and say in a whisper, "Anything I want and everything I need." My inclination when religious questions had arisen in the past was to slink away or change the subject. "Why did they kill Jesus?" she asked frequently, usually without any warning. "Hey, is that a dinosaur over there?" I might reply. "Don't you think it's time we got a puppy?" "Can I interest you in a cookie?" One night after dinner after McGowan's seminar, I tried deflecting the question to my visiting yet unsuspecting mother-in-law, who certainly knew the answer. "Why don't you ask Babo?" I said optimistically. Babo stared straight ahead and said nothing, no doubt uncomfortable that she might contradict our teaching, or nonteaching, on the matter, but this was straight from McGowan's playbook. He often directed his three children to take their inquiries about Christianity to his Southern Baptist mother-in-law. He believed the way to handle religious differences in an extended family was not to avoid or ignore them but to engage them respectfully. Acknowledge the legitimacy of their beliefs in the hopes they will do the same with yours. Humor their rituals and ask them to participate in yours. He even argued for letting trusted relatives take your children with them to church, which I had allowed my brother to do only once, and then quite warily. I don't know what I was afraid might happen, really. When they returned, I learned that during Sunday school, the teacher had asked why people go to church in the first place, and my son had eagerly raised his hand. "To sing!" he answered. Boy, did I feel dumb.

There was one subject on which McGowan dropped his commitment to teaching open-mindedness: hell. Hell, he said, is "a thought-stopper," a weapon used to injure reason. Instilling the fear of eternal damnation for failing to think in a certain way was "intellectual terrorism." He believed he had no choice but to ridicule the very notion of it. Hell had terrified him as a child, and it had taken him years to dissuade himself of that fear and realize that it was not just unlikely, but downright silly. So on this one topic, McGowan absolved himself of his responsibility to promote free inquiry. I wasn't sure how I felt about this. Of course, it appealed to my desire to shield my children from unnecessary fear. But I worried that his derision of hell and hell alone was the thread that would unravel his tightly wound argument for free-thought parenting. Wouldn't even the most rational-thinking Christians object to erasing this key concept while still claiming the mantle of open-mindedness? Of course, hell is a silly concept, but couldn't kids figure that out on their own? What was so special about hell?

My children, it turned out, had already been briefed on this one. Cristina had the same view as McGowan. Once, when an innocent reference to hell had appeared in one of their bedtime stories, the kids asked if it was real. She had quickly dismissed the notion and made it clear to me later that, like McGowan, she had no qualms about indoctrination in this one instance. They were not going to believe in hell any more than they were going to believe that if the aye-aye lemur at the primate center points a long, skinny middle finger at you, it's the kiss of death, as some people in its native Madagascar believe. One night recently, she was listening to our son read a book about sharks when he stopped abruptly and asked her again if hell was real. "No, it's not," Cristina said. "Why do you ask?" A little girl in his class had told him that "hell is in the ground and it will open up and eat you." He wasn't buying it. "I think she has been watching too many cartoons," he said with a smile. His mother agreed.

] [

After the seminar wrapped up, a group of us joined McGowan for dinner at a nearby Irish pub. As we were sitting down, his wife, Becca, handed him a cell phone so he could speak with his children before doing anything else, which he did at length and then told them good night. I asked him about the disdain many atheists have for religious moderates. Did he agree that people in the middle, on the fence, had a hand in the damage that religion does? No, he said. In fact, religious moderates have a lot in common with the nonreligious. But too often moderates sit silently while terrible things are done in the name of faith, McGowan said. He tells his middle-of-the-road friends that he's "doing the heavy lifting" in defense of reason and free inquiry. At the same time, he blanched at the intolerance of many in his own camp. He had atheist friends who got furious when he said that religion wasn't going to go away. The magician Penn Jillette, who was a contributor to *Parenting Beyond Belief*, ripped McGowan after a reference to "Christ-tards" was edited out of his essay. It was then that McGowan devised a brilliant name for the self-righteousness of some atheists: "Unholier than thou."

What about the old saw of moral relativism? I asked. Christians claim their moral standards are absolute because they come from on high and thus are superior to any code created by humans. McGowan dismissed the idea as nonsense. The Sixth Commandment, "Thou shalt not kill," is violated regularly in times of war. All morality is relative in that it is shaped by the circumstances under which it is applied, he said. That doesn't justify situational ethics, or following only the law of the wild, but it does argue against the notion that relativism is the exclusive domain of non-believers. Anyway, humans understand how to act in fundamentally moral ways. We just need encouragement, "an inclination to the good" he called it, and that's where parents come in. He cited studies showing that children, no matter whether they're raised in religious families or not, all develop empathy and kindness by a certain age. In fact, the surest way to impede that moral development was through, you guessed it, the thought-stopping of indoctrination. During the seminar, he had read a quote from a book for teens by Christian televangelist Joyce Meyer counseling them to be on the lookout for "questions planted by Satan": "I once asked the Lord why so many people are confused and He said to me, 'Tell them to stop trying to figure everything out, and they will stop being confused.'" The audience of unbelievers let forth with a frightened gasp at this ridiculous claptrap, and I started to feel that maybe the victim card I had noticed being played was warranted. "You have to look at this kind of thing and be determined to parent in the opposite direction," McGowan said, and I felt a brief swelling of pride in my humanist brethren. Throughout the seminar, Evangelicals, Southern Baptists, and other conservative Christians were repeatedly cited as members of an opposing team, but in a respectful way. It was the only time I saw McGowan call for fighting back, and it felt good when he did.

After two hours of talking over the growing din of the bar, the group parted ways, and I bundled up for the frigid hike back to my hotel. I was feeling affirmed. McGowan was not the stereotypical atheist obsessing about petty breaches of church and state. He was optimistic—about the growth of the nonreligious, the increasing acceptance of secular parenting, our ability to coexist with people of faith, and the future of society if freethinking is valued. I wished my parents could have met him. I sensed a self-assurance that I certainly lacked, and many of my contemporaries, too, who had opted out of the ready-made support and social acceptance that church provides, as Jay's mother had said. I had worried that by not sending me to church, not providing for a religious education, my parents had kept me on the outside looking in. But I was becoming a bit more comfortable with that choice. Maybe it was the one I would have made, the one I am making myself, for my own children, but also for me. Maybe that's all they were ever doing, too. I thought about my parents' decision to join a church following my brother's conversion, and their invitation to me to do the same. It had allowed me to see them dropping their guard, opening their mind, questioning past decisions, and trying to make a bad situation better. At least in that choice, they were modeling the détente that McGowan had called for and, without claiming that now, they somehow were in possession of truth or virtue or righteousness. They couldn't have known where their decisions regarding our upbringing would lead us as a family, but they had done their best and done it with honesty and integrity. Who was I to complain?

On a damp, frigid Sunday morning that weekend in the mountains, we stood in a circle with people we considered among our closest allies in adulthood. David read briefly from the Bible and offered thanks to above in a gentle tone that I would later come to know as his pastoral voice, and two other friends followed with poems. I stood beside him, holding the baby so he could sit up, and fighting back tears as I thought about how much love I had for this tiny person who weighed less than a Thanksgiving turkey, who spent most of his waking hours joined to my wife's chest, who had yet to utter a word or take a step or do much more than make regular deposits in his Huggies. Did I feel gratitude in the same way that Cristina did? I couldn't. He had not spent nine months inside my body, nor taken fourteen hours to come out, without incident. But I did now understand why she wanted us to perform this little ritual. It was a way to affirm the beauty of life in its raw, untainted, unadulterated state, a dangerous beauty, for sure, a life full of risks ahead, but beauty nonetheless. There was a phrase I had seen on a T-shirt that seemed to describe it: PURE POTENTIALITY. We had begun our lives anew with this boy's birth, been born again, as it were, as we would yet a second time two years later, and it seemed right to greet that new beginning with appreciation. To whom, exactly? I still don't know. For what, specifically? I'm equally clueless. I still can't bring myself to believe it was anything more than luck that he was such a perfect specimen from the day he was born, and that his sister was, too. But it seemed only fair at the time. Even today, the one thing I know that would shake my skepticism about the afterlife would be to lose either one of them.

Elizabeth, a dear friend who was with us that weekend, now married and the mother of luminous twin girls, sent out a card recently on which was printed this quote from Meister Eckhart, a fourteenth-century German mystic who believed in the holiness of all people: "If the only prayer you ever say in your whole life is 'thank you,' that would suffice." Nice, right? Of course, he was condemned as a heretic by Pope John XXII, so I'm not sure "thank you" actually did suffice in his case. I don't know if it would suffice in mine, either. But for my son, we said it on that cold November day, and as I write this, it occurs to me that

I might want to keep saying it, lest that someone or some-thing think I'm not just as appreciative of that gift today as I was on that day. Because I am. So thank you, whoever you are, whatever you are, wherever you are. I owe you one. Actually, make that two. That's my prayer.

Hey, it's a start.

ACKNOWLEDGMENTS

God bless Faye Bender, my stellar agent, who understood what I was trying to say even when I didn't.

Glory be to Rachel Holtzman, whose clear-eyed editing rescued me over and over, and to Megan Newman and the entire staff at Avery, and Jeff Galas.

Rejoice at the sound of Ron Stodghill for being that rare combination—friend and mentor.

Can I get an "Amen!" for Ewan and Kathy Park, who answered my questions with grace and aplomb and never failed to offer their love and support?

Say "Hallelujah!" for Oris Hubbard, Betty Thompson, and everyone else at the North Carolina Conference of the

International Pentecostal Holiness Church, for helping me understand Falcon, and for my late cousin Mayo Bundy, for writing the books that made me want to know more in the first place.

Keep Brian and Wesley Wilcox in your prayers, for welcoming me into their home and into their life.

To Ron and Carol Gestwicki for their generosity of time and spirit: Godspeed.

And for their vital intellectual, psychological, or material nourishment, and in some cases all three, thanks be to Brenda Alpinieri, Bill Bernstein, Derek Bing, May and Cotton Bryan, Scott and Gabi Culpepper, Elizabeth Davis and Scotty Utz, Julia Elliott, Jay Gestwicki, Carolyn Harris, Adam and Susan Jones, Dave and Susie Jones, Chris Keber, Jim Kirkland, Emily and David Lindsay, Murphy and Chuck Merrill, Ann Robbins, Mercedes Smith, Anne Smith, Anthony Smith, David Smith, Greg Smith, Pablo Sosa, Ainslie Uhl, Urlan Wannop, and Fred Webb.

Finally, praise Cristina Smith, the one from whom all my blessings flow.

ABOUT THE AUTHOR

Andrew Park is a former correspondent for *Business-Week*, whose work has also appeared in *The New York Times* and other national publications. He lives in Chapel Hill, North Carolina, with his wife, Cristina Smith, and their two children.